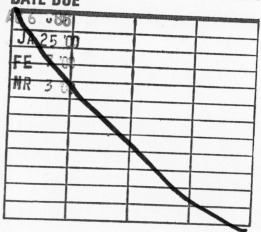

Strategy and Choice in Congressional Elections

Second Edition

GARY C. JACOBSON
AND
SAMUEL KERNELL

Yale University Press
New Haven and London

Designed by James J. Johnson
and set in Melior Roman.
Printed in the United States of America by
The Vail-Ballou Press, Binghamton, N.Y.

Library of Congress Cataloging in Publication Data

Jacobson, Gary C.
    Strategy and choice in congressional elections.

    Includes bibliographical references and index.
        1. United States. Congress—Elections.   2. Voting
—United States.   3. Politics, Practical.
4. Political psychology.   I. Kernell, Samuel,
1945-   II. Title.
JK1067.J32   324.7′2′097
ISBN 0–300–03135–1
ISBN 0–300–03077–0 pbk.

10   9   8   7   6   5   4   3   2   1

For Marty and Dianne

Contents

List of Tables

List of Figures

Preface

The theoretical insight that inspired this book came to us independently during separate and dissimilar research projects involving congressional elections. Finding ourselves impelled by quite different observations and perspectives toward the same theoretical conclusion, and discovering it to be rich with implications, we decided to give it a more comprehensive statement and to assemble the evidence in its favor. The result is this essay. Beyond an initial division of labor on the first draft, the work was completely shared, and we are jointly responsible for the whole.

At least, we are for its failings. Credit for its virtues is more broadly shared. Neal Beck, Peter Cowhey, John Mendeloff, Sandy Lakoff, and Sam Popkin, our colleagues at U.C. San Diego, alerted us to some important implications of the theory. Heinz Eulau, Morris Fiorina, Gerald Kramer, Jim Kuklinski, Thomas Mann, Aaron Wildavsky, and members of the Southern California Political Behavior Seminar offered valuable comments—and raised some sharp questions—about an earlier statement of the theory. If we remain entangled in the error of our ways, it is not through lack of smart criticism.

Susan Ehlinger, Judy Lyman, and Barbara Ziering typed and retyped our many drafts with patience and alacrity. The research for this book was supported by grants from the National Science Foundation (Kernell, SOC-78-18542; Jacobson, SES-80-7577), for which we are both grateful.

Finally, we thank our wives, Marty and Dianne, for keeping it all in perspective. This book is dedicated to them.

Preface to the Second Edition

The original edition of this book provoked a good deal of comment and discussion, just as we had hoped. We are grateful to everyone who has contributed to it. Special thanks are owed to Tom Mann and Catherine Rudder, whose request for an article on the 1982 election for the Summer 1982 *PS* led ultimately to the epilogue included in this edition.

1

Congressional Elections: Some Puzzling Contradictions

The 1974 election was a disaster for the Republican party. Republicans suffered a net loss of 43 seats in the U.S. House of Representatives, reducing their share to less than one third. The nationwide vote for Republican congressional candidates—41.1 percent—was the lowest for any party in this century. The party's misfortune was pervasive; state-level election returns were, if anything, worse. Prior to the election, Republicans held 41 percent of the seats in the state legislatures across the country; afterward, only 32 percent. The net result was that Democrats captured control of both state houses in 37 states, up from 28, while Republican-controlled states dropped from 16 to 4. The election left only 13 Republican governors.

The extraordinary election results befitted the events of that year. A slumping economy, the series of crimes and blunders lumped together under the generic term "Watergate," the collapse of the Nixon administration, and President Ford's September pardon of his disgraced predecessor were widely and understandably considered to be the main sources of the disaster. But despite the grand scale of both cause and effect, the 1974 election has remained a formidable puzzle to students of voting behavior, for, as we observe in the next chapter, surveys of voters turned up little evidence that attitudes toward Nixon, Watergate, or the economy had much influence on voters' preferences.

How could these highly salient and (for the Republican party) negative events fail to light up in voter surveys as "big" reasons for the election outcomes? The discrepancy between

general, entirely plausible explanations of election results and
the reasons behind individual voters' choices was particularly
striking in 1974, but it is by no means confined to that year. As
we shall see, this puzzling contradiction is a general phenomenon, and it inspired us to rethink congressional elections.

A familiar tenet of political folk wisdom is that national
events and conditions have an important effect on congressional and, to a lesser degree, state and local elections. Nation-
wide phenomena—recessions, unemployment, inflation, presidential triumphs or blunders, scandals, and popular or unpopular
presidential candidates—are widely believed to have a direct
impact on the electoral prospects of candidates for Congress.
This common notion has been subjected to a good deal of scholarly investigation during the past decade. From this work has
emerged an intriguing pattern of apparently inconsistent results
comparable to the Watergate anomaly. Macrolevel studies of the
association between national political conditions and electoral
trends regularly uncover strong, robust relationships of the kind
that conventional political wisdom would lead us to expect.
But the various survey studies of voters have found individual
representations of such phenomena to have an inconsistent,
weak, indirect, or even no effect on the vote choice. Other considerations—most notably voters' assessments of the particular
pair of candidates competing in the contest—appear to be vastly
more important.

We propose in this book a theory of congressional voting
and elections that reconciles these contradictory findings and
solves the Watergate puzzle. The theory takes as its point of
departure the important, though often underappreciated, fact
that congressional elections involve candidates and campaigns.
We argue that politically active elites—candidates and those
who recruit and finance them—provide a crucial connecting
link between national-level phenomena and individual voting
decisions. National political conditions systematically shape
elite decisions about running for office or contributing to campaigns. These decisions determine the alternatives presented to
voters. Voters who must choose between two candidates will

favor attractive candidates who run well-financed campaigns. In this way, even those voters who are blissfully free of any concerns with national political issues may, in voting on the basis of bumper stickers and billboards, contribute to a national electoral swing by reflecting in their votes the advantages that accrue to the political party favored by national political conditions. The strategic decisions of politicians so structure the vote choice that electoral results are consonant with national-level forces even if individual voting decisions are not.

Some voters do, of course, express opinions on national issues or personal circumstances connected with national conditions in their votes and in their support of candidates. The microlevel relationships are, as we observe in chapter 2, not wholly barren. Moreover, such voters are most often found among the more active and articulate members of the electorate—to whom politicians are especially attentive. For these reasons, the electoral effects of national conditions are not merely the self-fulfillment of prophecies that guide strategic elite decisions. The prophecies are, rather, self-reinforcing; the preferences of some voters merge with the behavior of politicians to produce interpretable election outcomes.

In defense of our theory we undertake a close examination of the behavior of different classes of politicians to demonstrate that choices regarding candidacy do indeed reflect the national political environment. Chapters 3, 4, and 5 explore the forward-looking strategic calculations of challengers, incumbents, and contributors—the core participants of congressional campaigns. That elites respond strategically to their spring expectations about the fall elections does not in itself demonstrate that their actions contribute to the election outcome. Anticipated responses may, after all, be merely advanced artifacts of the election. But the evidence we present describes such a pervasive and consistent system of strategic elite responses that, given survey evidence of the crucial importance of candidates and campaigns for individual voting choices, the inference that cumulative elite strategies must affect aggregate election returns at the margin is unavoidable.

At this level our case is too circumstantial to be fully persuasive, however; we need more direct evidence that our theory actually provides a fuller explanation of congressional elections. The second task, then, is to offer some direct tests of the theory against macrolevel theories that assume, explicitly or by implication, an electorate that responds rationally to individual-level analogs of national events and conditions. This is begun at the end of chapter 5, but the real face-off between these theories, which we label in shorthand "economic voting," and our own comes in chapter 6.

In chapter 7 we examine the 1980 congressional elections from the perspective of our theory. As in 1974, the dramatic numbers—a shift of 12 seats to the Republican side in the Senate, giving them a majority for the first time in a generation, and the Republican gain of 33 seats in the House, several at the expense of prominent senior Democrats—have quickly been interpreted as the repudiation of an administration and punishment for economic failures, or, more radically, as a sharp national move to the right and the beginnings of a basic realignment of the electorate. Our theory supports a rather different interpretation.

Chapter 8 explores some implications of the theory for the operation of a representative democracy.

The 1982 elections, coming a year after the original edition of this book was published, provided a unique opportunity to test our approach against the more conventional referendum models. In the epilogue, newly prepared for this edition, we use the theory to explain why Republican losses were much smaller than expected from the deep recession and low ratings of the administration.

The first necessity, however, is to document more thoroughly the serious discrepancy between the theories of voting underlying aggregate studies and the manifest behavior of individual voters; this is our purpose in chapter 2.

2

Conflicting Theories of Congressional Elections

Organization Democrats far and near acted as if they were ashamed of their own President. His name was barely mentioned in speeches and campaign literature. With an eye to the Gallup polls, which indicated a drop in Mr. Truman's popularity from a honeymoon percentage of 87 percent to an October brown of 32 percent, they decided then he was to be written off as a loss. Republicans made the most of him as an issue.[1]

The power of the "pocketbook" issue was shown more clearly perhaps in 1958 than in any off-year election in history. On the international front, the Administration had had one of its best years. Yet, the economic dip in October was obviously uppermost in the people's minds when they went to the polls. They completely rejected the President's appeal for the election of Republicans to the House and Senate.[2]

The basic ideas represented by these two observations—that the popular status of the president and the state of the economy have an important influence on voters in congressional elections—have been stated more formally and given a variety of empirical tests by academic students of American elections. Two important lines of inquiry have been actively pursued during recent years. One approach treats elections as aggregate phenomena. Econometric techniques are employed to relate variations in election results nationally to aggregate measures of politically relevant conditions holding at the time of the election. The state of the economy, variously measured by the unemployment rate, inflation rate, or real income, is the explanatory variable common to this body of research. The other approach takes the individual voter rather than the national electorate as the unit of analysis. Sample surveys are used to examine respondents' perceptions and evaluations of political conditions—including, prominently, those pertaining to the economy—and their connection to the voting decision. Despite the recent abundance, indeed surfeit, of published research using each approach, the anomaly identified in chapter 1 is no closer to resolution. Indeed, with each new study reconciliation seems more problematic.

A third popular line of inquiry, inspired by an interest in explaining why incumbent congressmen win reelection so easily, has added to the confusion. Although no one has, to our knowledge, attempted to defend or reject economic theories of voting from its perspective, this research does, by inference, offer reasons to expect national conditions to be relatively unimportant as political issues. Incumbents seem to have learned how to insulate themselves quite effectively from national political forces. After a brief review of each of these approaches to understanding congressional elections, we suggest how the findings of the "incumbency" research provide an important clue to resolving the anomalous micro- and macrolevel conclusions.

POLITICAL CONDITIONS AND CONGRESSIONAL ELECTIONS: AGGREGATE STUDIES

With one important exception, to be examined below, the aggregate, time-series studies examine the relationship between some operational measures of the economy and the partisan division of the national congressional vote. Beginning with Gerald Kramer's seminal study in 1971,[3] most of the accumulated evidence is consistent with the notion that congressional elections are strongly influenced by economic conditions. This general conclusion does not imply the absence of important differences and disagreements between these numerous studies. Repeatedly, decisions involving thorny methodological issues have been found to affect substantive relationships. Investigators must decide which economic indices to use, whether the level of or the change in the index better represents the economy (and if the change, over what time period), whether to measure the congressional vote as a percentage of the total vote or of the two-party vote, and which time period to include. Their choices are important, for they alter the substantive conclusions supported by the research.

The diversity of approaches has its beneficial aspects, however. For one, a great deal of useful follow-up and replication research has been spawned. The enterprise almost looks like science.[4] And as a second-order consequence, this unusually large volume and variety of research provides a limited form of multimethod validation of the overall finding that congressional elections are sensitive to economic conditions. Even some of the studies that wish to deny or at least depreciate the relationship contribute to this general conclusion. Stigler, for example, in arguing a negative case, presents numerous "conservative" specifications, most of which produce results supportive of the overall claim of a systematic relationship between the economy and congressional elections.[5]

Edward Tufte contributed another dimension to this line of research by adding a measure of popular attitudes toward the president to the standard economic analysis.[6] His study makes the most persuasive case yet that the economy and national politics shape congressional elections. Tufte finds that the national division of the two-party, midterm congressional vote can be explained, statistically, as a linear, additive function of two variables, one economic and one political. Change in per capita, real disposable income over the preceding year and the president's job-performance rating in the Gallup poll in September together explain about 90 percent of the variance in the mid-term vote since 1938. Impressive stuff, but in chapter 6 we shall use our theory to try to improve upon his relationships.

Although, as Tufte cautions, "many different models of the underlying electorate are consistent with electoral outcomes that are collectively rational,"[7] the fact remains that aggregate election results are no more than the sum of individual prefer-ences. In the absence of alternative models, the reductionism from collective rationality to voter rationality is a seductive in-ference. Explicitly or implicitly, these studies have assumed that the economy and evaluations of the administration gener-ate their aggregate effects directly through their standing as im-portant issues for voters. Accepting Downs's version of the ra-tional, self-interested voter,[8] Kramer, for example, assumes

> that a decision rule of the following type is operative: if the performance of the incumbent party is "satisfactory" ac-cording to some simple standard, the voter votes to retain the incumbent governing party in office to enable it to con-tinue its present policies; while if the incumbent's perform-ance is not "satisfactory," the voter votes against the incum-bent, to give the opposition party a chance to govern.[9]

This theory of congressional elections, which we shall call "economic voting," is an entirely plausible representation of the electorate. Its only problem is that studies of individual voters provide so little supporting evidence.

POLITICAL CONDITIONS AND CONGRESSIONAL ELECTIONS: INDIVIDUAL VOTERS

The aggregate-level findings—and their underlying assump-tions—have directed attention to the influence of the economy on individual voting decisions. The studies published so far disagree mainly on which conceptualization of the economy is most relevant. Steven Weatherford prefaces his own analysis by sorting out four different forms economic variables may take, any or all of which may separately shape votes: personal financial experiences and expectations; perceptions of general economic conditions; evaluations of the government's economic performance; and party images on economic policies.[10]

Although Kramer's assumption is so broad that any of the first three representations of the economy would be appropriate, elsewhere in his article he clearly implies that personal financial well-being is the primary concern of the rational, "self-interested" voter. Economists Francisco Arcelus and Allan H. Meltzer flatly stipulate that "rational voters are concerned with their real income and real wealth."[11] Moreover, throughout this research, aggregate economic variables (e.g., percent unemployed) are designed to measure direct economic effects upon individual citizens.

The difficulty with the notion that the economy influences the vote through its effect on personal finances is that it receives almost no support from studies of individual voting behavior. This is in fact one of the few consistent findings in this literature.[12] The lengths to which one must go to find such a connection is exemplified by Morris P. Fiorina's ingenious exercise aiming to show that personal economic experiences "affect more general economic performance judgements, both types of judgements feed into evaluations of presidential performance, and the more general judgements, at least, contribute to the modifications of party identification," and presidential evaluations and party identification influence the vote.[13] But even if this elaborate construction is accepted—the plausible reverse causal sequence burdens the argument at several junctures—the effects are not large and the relationships barely reach conventional levels of statistical significance despite a large number of observations.

These same studies do produce evidence lending support to one or another of the alternative ways in which economic conditions might affect individual votes. But the reported effects are almost always rather small and the economic variables explain little additional variance in the vote once other variables are taken into account. Only voters' assessments of the relative economic competence of the two parties are regularly connected in an important way with the voting decision. And in this case, the variables are conceptually so similar that one may reasonably ask, What has been explained?

The electoral effects of voters' presidential evaluations are more consistent with aggregate research findings, although the strength of the connection varies from study to study (or from election to election). One of us (Kernell) found solid evidence that assessments of the president affect off-year congressional voters; the influence is strongest on voters who disapprove of the president's performance: negative voting.[14] One reason evaluation of the president's job performance is generally more closely related to the vote than are the economic variables is that it is a summary measure of the net effect of all politically relevant conditions, including the economy. Moreover, because the president is widely recognized to be the leader of his party, presidential evaluations are conceptually similar to vote choices.

Although presidential popularity is independently associated with the vote, there is, paradoxically, little evidence that the Watergate scandal had a significant political impact on voters. Despite the conspicuous Republican disaster in 1974 (documented in chapter 1) studies of individual voters did not find much of Watergate in the individual voting decision. Using the 1974 Center for Political Studies (CPS) National Election Study, but quite different analytical techniques (normal vote and multiple regression analysis, respectively), both Miller and Glass[15] and Conway and Wyckoff[16] reached the same conclusion. "Watergate and the distrust in government it fostered was not the most important factor in the Democratic landslide of 1974."[17] Watergate's effects were "indirect and complex" and, it should be added, very weak in both House and Senate voting decisions.[18] A much smaller and more limited Wisconsin study also discovered no differences in turnout or voting decisions that could be attributed to Watergate.[19]

In addition to the substantive reconciliation of these findings provided by our theory, we should note that cross-sectional survey research may mask some real direct effects of national forces on individual voting in several ways. For one, survey analysis commonly focuses upon the explanatory power of variables across individuals. It generally ignores the fact that minor individual-level relationships which work systematically in the same direction across electoral units may produce large marginal changes in the aggregate relationships over time. As Donald Kinder and Roderick Kiewiet put it,

> an extremely predictable aggregate phenomenon can be produced by modest individual-level relationships. If only a subset of all voters take into account their own economic circumstances in deciding which candidate to support, for example, or if all voters do but weigh other considerations more heavily, such conditions may nevertheless translate into very strong relationships between economic conditions and political decisions in the aggregate.[20]

Kernell aggregated the skewed effects of the presidential evaluations on congressional voting and found that a 9 percentage point change in the percent approving the president's job performance affected his party's congressional vote by 1.4 percentage points.[21] Tufte, in the aggregate-level study described above, similarly estimated that a 9 point change in popularity produced a 1.2 percentage point impact upon his party's vote. The agreement of these estimates strongly suggests a direct effect of presidential popularity on the marginal variations in congressional voting. For the economy, however, the individual-level relationships between personal financial well-being and the vote are so puny no one, to our knowledge, has bothered to attempt to assess their potential aggregate impact.

Cross-sectional studies may also mask some effects of national forces because these are always measured with individual partisanship controlled. If a portion of the electorate shifts its party allegiance in response to economic conditions or national scandals, a single cross-sectional sample will not pick up the shift. The close connection between marginal changes in the distribution of partisans and marginal changes in the two-party vote for House candidates makes it clear that this possibility must be taken seriously. The change in the proportion of Democratic identifiers reported in the SRC/CPS surveys from 1956 through 1978 is correlated at .67 with the change in the Democratic share of the national two-party vote.

Since we know that "leaning" partisans are as likely to change allegiance as are weak partisans,[22] but are more likely to change their party affiliation between elections,[23] we have one obvious explanation for this connection. A small, but not trivial, segment of the electorate attaches itself, in response to interviewers' questions, to the party whose candidate it intends to support. If both the vote and party choice are a response to national forces, real longitudinal effects can exist without revealing themselves in cross-sectional studies.

And last, it may simply be that the cross-sectional variance in response to variables is idiosyncratic while the cross-temporal variance—that is, between observations or surveys—is systematic. In this case a series of cross-sectional surveys may fail to detect any relationships of the variable with the vote while a regression analysis of the aggregate relationships over the same time period could produce striking results. Kramer has demonstrated that stong, underlying individual relationships may appear either nonexistent or oppositely directed in the standard cross-sectional analyses.[24]

Panel data theoretically allow us to tap this cross-temporal relationship at the individual level of analysis. Although more work needs to be performed in this area, the existing panel studies do not suggest that this distinction between cross-temporal and cross-sectional reconciles the important substantive differences in individual- and aggregate-level research.

Fiorina's work, mentioned earlier, uses panel data and estimation techniques which allow economic and political variables to operate through their effect on party identification as well as directly on the vote. Even so, only variables reflecting opinions of presidential performance, not those measuring assessments of national or personal economic conditions, can be interpreted as influencing the congressional vote in 1976.[25]

Richard Brody's work with the 1972–1974 CPS panel shows that changes in the direction of party affiliation reported by some respondents were linked to their attitudes towards Nixon and to personal economic experiences. But one can calculate from the data he presents that the net effect of these variables amounts to, at most, a 2.2 percentage point shift toward the Democratic party; the actual shift was about 6 percentage points nationally, more than 5 in the panel sample. The evidence he offers from the 1956–1958 panel shows individual economic changes to have had an even smaller effect, accounting for, at most, a shift of 1.6 percentage points in favor of the Democrats in a year when the actual shift was 5.2 percentage points (4.6 in the sample).[26]

With the partial exception of presidential job evaluations, the results of individual-level studies of congressional voting have not conformed to the assumptions or expectations arising from the aggregate studies. In particular, a good, rational, economic vote is hard to find. An undertone of disappointment is discernible in many of the reports of this research.

THE IMPACT OF INCUMBENCY IN CONGRESSIONAL ELECTIONS

A third important body of work—one which has enjoyed greater success in explaining vote preferences but which in doing so has undermined the economic voting theory—investigates the electoral advantages of congressional incumbency.[27] Weakening partisanship, candidate-centered mass-media campaigns, the explosive growth of congressional "perks," and, according to Burnham, the lack of structure in public attitudes on important political issues[28] have rendered the connections between national events and congressional elections ever more tenuous. This would not in itself contradict the conclusions drawn from macro political research—if the marginal effects of the systematic variables were sufficiently large—but it certainly adds to the burden that the economic voting theory must bear.

More damaging to that theory is the insight this research has given us into the primary components of the individual voting decisions. Evidence has accumulated that what matters most to voters is the choice offered by the particular pair of candidates in the district. This requires an important revision of accepted theories of congressional voting behavior. The pioneering work of Donald Stokes and Warren Miller,[29] reinforced by later research[30] found most voters to be ignorant of congressional candidates and issues and dependent upon party and other simple cues (incumbency, remembering the candidates' names, feelings about the president) to guide the voting decision. Since so little was known of the candidates—about half the voters regularly forget the name of the House candidate they voted for[31]—visible national forces such as the state of the economy and opinions about the president would seem to have ample opportunity to influence voting.

The national surveys used in almost all of this research (the series of SRC/CPS National Election Studies) provided some early clues that more complex phenomena were operating. For example, respondents reported voting more for incumbents than for challengers even if they could not recall their names[32]—a mysterious finding if simple name recall is all that is involved. Alan Abramowitz discovered that respondents in one Oregon congressional district could evaluate candidates quite readily without remembering their names, and more significantly, that these evaluations were the most important determinants of their votes.[33] One of us (Jacobson) reported similar findings about 1974 Senate voters.[34] Thomas Mann clarified the issue by showing that voters were able to *recognize* candidates' names (which is all they have to do in the voting booth) much more readily than they could *recall* them and that recognition of candidates was accompanied by assessments of their (mainly personal) virtues and defects, which had a strong impact on the vote quite apart from the voter's party identification.[35]

The idea that voters' evaluations of the particular candidates are crucially important in determining their preferences has been given overwhelming support by the 1978 CPS National Election Study. This study contains the most comprehensive information available on congressional voting with a large number of new questions and an additional set of contextual data on the districts in which sample respondents resided. A consistent finding reported in early papers exploiting these data is that voters' assessments of the two candidates are at least as important as party attachments in determining how people vote and that these assessments are vastly more important than any other factor.[36] Specifically, incumbents do so well because they are well known and, what is more important, well liked; their challengers do so poorly because they are obscure and held in low regard.

The incumbents' greater renown and attractiveness are the primary source of the incumbency advantage; this becomes clear when the components of the vote choice are understood. Consider the two regression equations in table 2.1.[37] The first treats the vote as a function of variables conventionally found to be important: the voter's party identification, familiarity with the candidates, and the incumbency status of the candidates. All of these theoretically important variables have a statistically significant impact on the vote, and together they account for half the overall variance in the sample's preferences.

The second equation adds a set of variables representing voters' assessments of the candidates: whether or not they like or dislike something about each. The regression estimates suggest that the incumbency and familiarity variables are largely surrogates for voters' evaluations of the candidates. Each of the four evaluative variables has a strong and separable impact on the vote; something liked or disliked changes the probability of voting for the Democrat by from .157 to .316 independently of other factors. Collectively, these variables account for an impressive 30 percent of the variance; the second most important factor, party identification, accounts for only 17 percent. All the variables together explain 62 percent of the variance in the vote.[38]

TABLE 2.1. Regression Models of the Voting Decision: 1978 House Elections

	Regression Coefficient	t Ratio	Beta[a]
Dependent Variable			
Respondent's vote (N = 873)			
Independent Variables			
Equation 2.1			
Party identification	.210	16.03	.40
Democrat is incumbent	.142	3.67	.14
Republican is incumbent	−.153	−3.76	−.15
Familiarity with Democrat	.098	5.38	.15
Familiarity with Republican	−.151	−8.13	−.25
Constant	.542		
R^2 = .50			
Equation 2.2			
Party identification	.156	13.04	.30
Democrat is incumbent	.060	1.74	.06
Republican is incumbent	−.055	−1.39	−.05
Familiarity with Democrat	.073	4.09	.11
Familiarity with Republican	−.099	−5.55	−.16
Likes something about Democrat	.199	7.49	.19
Dislikes something about Democrat	−.189	−6.18	−.14
Likes something about Republican	−.316	−10.40	−.30
Dislikes something about Republican	.157	4.81	.11
Constant	.578		
R^2 = .62			

SOURCE: 1978 NES/CPS National Election Study.
[a]Standardized regression coefficient.

The point of this literature for any theory of national conditions and electoral change is plain. The dominant components of the individual voting decision are the voter's opinions about the candidates running in the district. In 1978, at least, voters' feelings about President Carter and ratings of his job performance had little appreciable effect on the congressional vote once these other variables were taken into account.[39] The same is true of voters' opinions about how effectively the government was handling the problems of inflation and unemployment. The voters focused upon the choices in front of them rather than upon broad national issues.

An additional point established by the 1978 study, which will become relevant to our discussion in the next chapter, is that the very high rate of success enjoyed by House incumbents is basically a consequence of weak opposition.[40] They are re-elected easily because, in most cases, they are not opposed by attractive, adequately publicized challengers. At the district level, the outcome of the election depends in large part on the electoral choice presented to the voters by a particular pair of candidates. In races involving incumbents, the quality of the challenger and the vigor of his campaign turn out to be the crucial variables.[41]

DISTRICT LEVEL VARIABLES VS. NATIONAL POLITICAL FORCES

The problem survey studies pose for any theory associating elections with national political conditions is that district-level forces explain so much of the individual vote choice and national-level forces so little. From the perspective of those seeking to understand the sources of electoral change, this last body of research appears to reveal idiosyncracy run amok. But does it? Can these findings be reconciled with—indeed, even inform—the equally robust, but substantively different, findings from aggregate-level research? This question has been ignored by those engaged in hot pursuit of the sources of the incumbency advantage. And those developing the aggregate economic voting models have explicitly denied the need for such a linkage. In light of these recent findings, Kramer's 1971 argument, for example, appears mistaken:

> Although individual races may deviate from the overall pattern, in general it seems that most Congressional candidates appear to most voters simply as Democrats or Republicans, and not as clearly defined personalities with their

own policy views and records; and hence, variations in the overall popularity of the parties should be a major factor in producing short-term fluctuations in the Congressional vote.[42]

Four years later Arcelus and Meltzer were not claiming that candidates and campaigns are unimportant but that they are irrelevant to the aggregate-level research because, "local issues and personalities . . . [are] assumed to be independent of aggregate economic variables."[43] And Bloom and Price, while conceding that "candidate personalities may play an important role," concluded that, "as long as they are not correlated with income changes their omission does not bias resulting estimates of the impact of economic conditions on the vote."[44] We believe that the assumptions that candidates and campaigns are idiosyncratic, should cancel out across districts, and are otherwise unrelated to national-level forces are dead wrong. In the next chapter we demonstrate, from commonly accepted notions about elite political behavior, why this must be so.

3

Strategic Politicians

V. O. Key felt it necessary to argue in his last book that "voters are not fools."[1] Neither, we contend, are politicians. Their career plans and decisions are strategically adapted to the political environment. National political forces which politicians expect to have some impact on voters shape their election plans. As a result, the relative quality of a party's candidates and the vitality of their campaigns—the things which have the strongest impact on individual voters—are not at all independent of national events and conditions. Rather, they are a direct function of them. This has important implications for understanding how aggregate national phenomena affect aggregate election outcomes. The crucial links, we will show, are provided by strategic politicians.

THE OPPORTUNITY STRUCTURE

Electoral politics in America is a competitive business. The demand for political offices is greater than the supply. Yet this oversupply of ambitious politicians does not make an election a free-for-all. Instead, competition for public office tends to be structured and orderly; candidates sort themselves out among the many offices in a predictable fashion. In some political systems the coordination of politicians and offices is performed centrally through strong party organizations that recruit candidates and direct careers. In the United States this coordination is a product of individual politicians behaving strategically—

19

that is, looking out for their own best interest—within a commonly perceived structure that offers advantages and incentives for political mobility.

The marketplace for political office is structured, but not overly so. The plethora of offices, peculiar to America, invites a large number of potential competitors, provides numerous opportunities for mobility, and raises some uncertainty about the prospects for success. Under these circumstances successful politicians must be acutely strategic in making career choices. How the structure of opportunities determines the targets and, more importantly, the timing of career moves has important implications for a theory that views the collective strategic behavior of politicians as an important determinant of election outcomes.

A central element of the structure of political opportunities is the stratification of offices. Only in the most poorly developed political system would one expect to find all institutional offices equally desirable (or, more accurately in such an instance, undesirable). Since the late nineteenth century, public offices in America have been ranked into a loose but widely acknowledged hierarchy with more attractive offices fewer in number and competition for them stiffer.[2] At the top of the heap is the presidency; next are seats in the Senate and governorships; below these are the somewhat more numerous seats in the House of Representatives; and at the bottom lie a multitude of state legislative and local offices. Some offices do not fit neatly into this sequence; consider the careers of recent New York City mayors. And from state to state the ranking of offices, especially at the lower rungs, will vary considerably, depending upon such factors as the size of the office's constituency, the number of offices available, and the office's value as a stepping-stone to higher offices. Nonetheless, the general pattern adequately describes the sequence of offices sought by most politicians across the nation.

In addition to stratifying offices, the opportunity structure guides the strategic behavior of politicians in a couple of other ways. First, it institutionalizes competition, making politicians cautious risk-takers. The pyramidal distribution of offices eases the entry of men and women into public life but, as they attempt to move up the hierarchy, the steady attrition of offices creates competition and uncertainty for all politicians, including the incumbents. Second, the opportunity structure differentially allocates resources among offices within levels such that transitions from one status level of offices to the next is nonrandom. Certain officeholders are favored by virtue of their current position in seeking some target office. Over time, these advantages define highly visible career paths. The linkage of offices across levels reflects, to use Joseph Schlesinger's term, their "manifest" similarities.[3] For one thing, the structural isomorphism of national and state governments creates functionally similar offices throughout the hierarchy. From justice of the peace to the Supreme Court and from the state house to the U.S. Senate, offices at different levels are associated by similar tasks. This makes some officeholders at a lower level more plausible, hence advantaged, successors to a higher office than others.

The federal tiering of the office hierarchy also introduces a network of overlapping constituencies. Congressional districts, for example, generally subsume several state legislative districts and are in turn subsumed within the Senate's statewide constituency. With upward political mobility in America largely occurring through sequential capturing and expanding of constituencies, the politician's current office becomes an important vehicle for career advancement.

At first glance an opportunity structure that produces many more aspirants for Congress than there are seats available would appear to guarantee that there will always be well-qualified (politically experienced) candidates within each party trying to get the nomination.[4] If so, this would support the conventional assumption, noted in the preceding chapter, that the quality of candidates will be constant in the aggregate and therefore can be ignored in explaining the national congressional vote. Upon closer inspection, however, the opportunity structure yields two general conclusions which together deny the assumption of consistent candidate quality.

First, we note that because of dissimilar institutional resources even within ranks, some politicians make better candidates for a target office than others. This in itself is not a profound observation but it does lead to the second point. To the
degree a politician's current office is a resource for advancement, it becomes a stake or risk in considering whether and
when to attempt a move. Offices have investment value beyond
whatever intrinsic rewards they provide their occupants. Even
the politician who serves in an office solely to enhance his future mobility must plan carefully the timing of his move. The
institutional advantages provided by the opportunity structure
mean that running and losing, and in the process losing one's
office base, not only interrupts a career, but well may end it.

THE STRATEGIC CALCULUS

A base office as a resource inspires ambition but as a stake it
urges caution. To appreciate better how politicians resolve their
dilemma and how the decision to seek some higher office relates
to partisan electoral conditions, consider Gordon Black's formal
statement of the upwardly mobile politician's decision calculus:[5]

Equation 3.1

$$U_o = (PB) - R,$$

where

U_o = utility of target office O,
P = probability of winning election to Office O,
B = value of Office O,
R = risk (e.g., cost of campaign, intrinsic value of base office, opportunity cost of losing base office).

According to this formulation, if the value of target Office O (B)
discounted by the probability of victory (P) is greater than the
cost of seeking the office (R), the utility of seeking the office (U_o)
is positive and the politician becomes a candidate.

In explaining variations in the quality of congressional candidacies over a series of elections the main message of this equation is that the more the politician risks, the greater must be the probability of winning before he or she becomes a candidate. Stakes vary widely among potential candidates, reflecting their position in the opportunity structure, and therefore so too will the electoral conditions necessary to trigger their candidacy. The political neophyte wishing to go straight to Congress risks little more than the personal cost of the campaign; even a low likelihood of success may not deter the attempt. The seasoned state senator whose district represents a large chunk of the congressional district, however, will await optimal political conditions before cashing in his investment.

The collective result of these individual calculations can be viewed as an equilibrium process, diagrammed in figure 3.1. Since the base office is both a stake and resource, the quality (Q) of a party's congressional challengers will be a function of its perceived probability (P) of winning the fall elections. And since Democratic and Republican electoral fortunes are inversely related to each other, short-term partisan forces will have opposite motivational impact on prospective Democratic and Republican candidates. The more extreme the electoral climate, the greater will be the divergence between the parties in the overall quality of their candidates.

FIGURE 3.1   The Quality of a Party's Congressional Challengers as a
Function of Its Electoral Prospects

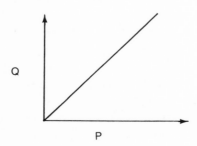

The discussion of individual voting decisions in chapter 2 implies that the better a party's candidates, the better its performance in the election. Given the relationship described in figure 3.1, the collective strategic choices of politicians to become candidates reinforce and augment the effects of the current political environment on the election. These decisions determine, in aggregate, the kinds of candidates and campaigns voters are offered in an election year. National events and conditions shape the expectations of potential candidates and their supporters about their party's electoral prospects. Their expectations affect their strategies and thus their behavior. And this, in turn, structures the choices voters are offered in districts across the nation. The election outcome becomes in part the aggregate consequence of many politicians individually making strategic decisions about their political careers. In this way, macroelectoral behavior can be derived directly from straightforward features of the opportunity structure.

AN ALTERNATIVE COLLECTIVE STRATEGY

One need not look too hard at figure 3.1 to discover an alternative strategy for political parties facing an unfavorable political environment. If they were somehow able to reverse the relationship so that unfavorable conditions were greeted with high quality candidacies, they would minimize the effects of adverse political conditions upon the vote. The party's collective goal of minimizing the loss of congressional seats serves the interest of every loyal congressman, especially when the threatened losses would reduce his party to minority status.[6] As attractive as this alternative strategy may be for promoting the party's collective goals, it is nonetheless unavailable, for it requires individual politicians to behave in direct contradiction to their own self-interest. The provision of collective goods requires collective action. Strong political parties which centrally coordinate candidacies and campaigns by sanctioning reluctants and compensating victims of defeat may have such a strategy as an option.

But the weak American party system and the evolved opportunity structure guarantee that politicians will be entrepreneurs and that only the individually calculated relationship described in figure 3.1 will occur.

CONGRESSIONAL INCUMBENTS

Although the net result of the aggregated individual strategic decisions should be to accentuate the relationship between the partisan political climate and election results, it is not obvious that all strategic decisions relating to congressional candidacies and campaigns must have this effect. With the strategic calculus in equation 3.1 describing the choice to leave one office and seek another, the discussion thus far best applies to nonincumbent congressional candidates. How well can this equation be adapted to depict the calculus of the incumbent congressman content with his position and ambitious only to protect it? Moreover, do incumbents' strategic responses to political conditions have the same multiplier effect on elections? We think that they do.

Every two years the incumbent congressman must decide whether to seek reelection (most do), to run for higher office, or to retire. Although this last choice is more often subject to nonstrategic considerations, it can similarly be couched in strategic terms. A decision to stand for reelection rather than seek a Senate seat (PB) will generally reflect the unacceptable cost (R) involved in giving up the House seat to make the attempt. In considering whether to run for reelection or to retire, the risk term is greatly discounted since in both instances the "risk" involves losing the House seat. Understandably, most congressmen in any given year run for reelection. So many run so successfully that the incumbency effect has emerged in recent years as an overwhelming deterrent to quality challengers. After many years in Congress, however, each additional two-year term may grow marginally less attractive (B) and at some point when confronted with adverse political conditions (P) and a tough campaign (R) the senior congressman will "strategically" retire. Because incumbents have been winning reelection at an 85 percent clip or better since the late nineteenth century,[7] retirement decisions should, of course, be relatively resistant to short-term partisan conditions. We show in chapter 5, however, that partisan retirement rates are in fact marginally associated with election year political conditions.

Threatened with the prospect of defeat, most incumbent congressmen who are not near retirement will redouble their campaign effort in order to minimize the effects of unfavorable political conditions. Ostensibly, such behavior contradicts our theory. The quality of the candidacies appears to improve the more severe the threat. But the redoubled efforts of incumbents drain resources from party candidates running for open seats or those challenging vulnerable opposition incumbents. Because these resources are far more effective when used in the campaigns of nonincumbents, this collective "circle-the-wagons" strategy becomes self-defeating. We shall return to this argument in the next chapter.

Suppliers of campaign resources also act strategically. Decisions about how much to give to whom are guided by perceptions of national conditions. Contributors' strategies, like those of politicians, accentuate the advantages of the favored party. The financial connection is, in fact, so important to our theory that in the next chapter we provide a separate discussion of the strategic calculus and aggregate behavior of contributors.

STRATEGIC POLITICIANS: READING TEA LEAVES

This account of political strategies is, we believe, intuitively compelling, but of course its validity depends on how well it coincides with the actual behavior of politicians. A variety of data suggests that politicians do think and act strategically, with consequences that match those predicted by our theory.

If, to begin, congressional elections are largely the product of strategic politicians making choices in anticipation of the outcome, then we should expect to find current and prospective officeholders showing more than passing curiosity in signs about their party's electoral prospects. They do. Potential participants in congressional campaigns begin assessing the prevailing breezes well before the election—and before the final decisions about candidacy have to be made. There are plenty of possible indicators from which to choose.

Published speculation about what will happen in the fall is common in the first few months of an election year. Examples are easy to find. In 1946, the *New York Times* reported in January that Truman's troubles with reconversion legislation, which had put him at odds with important Democrats in Congress, had left "many Democrats . . . dismayed over [its] effects in both 1946 (Congressional) and 1948 (presidential and Congressional) elections."[8] In February, the *Times* was reporting that the outlook for Republicans was the best in 13 years,[9] and by March, Republican leaders were claiming that "there was no question on the basis of nation-wide reports but that the party would carry the House this year and very likely the Senate."[10] Democrats were admitting privately that their chances were poor in light of public dissatisfaction with the administration's economic performance in readjusting the nation to a peacetime economy.

In 1958 it was the Republicans' turn to worry. The Soviet Union's launching of Sputnik in 1957, followed by a recession which deepened in the early months of 1958, heartened Democratic politicians. Their leaders exuded confidence, claiming as early as February that "in the November election at least half a dozen new Democratic seats would be gained in the Senate and a minimum of fifty in the House."[11] Democratic optimism was matched by Republican gloom. Early in February *Newsweek* reported the following exchange:

> Rep. Gerald Ford of Michigan tried to find a hopeful note. Personally, said Ford, he doubted that the GOP's losses would be as serious as some of the others thought. "I'll bet you five dollars," responded Rep. Walter Norblad of Oregon, "that we lose at least 30 seats." Ford took the bet, but it

was all too clear from the faces of his colleagues that they thought he would lose it.[12]

In both instances, a poor economy and the administration's inability to deal with it effectively were the sources of partisan joy or depression. In other years, however, the president emerged as the central issue either as an asset or liability for his party. One year was 1962. The *New York Times* speculated in February that rather than the normal increase in congressional seats in the off year, the opposition Republican party faced the problem of "how to avoid being ground deeper into the minority this fall. . . . [It] is confronted with a Democratic president whose personal popularity is at a record peak, who commands a near monopoly over the headlines and who has recently shown both zest and skill for putting the Republicans on the political spot."[13] "It looks too good too early," one wary Democrat observed in April.[14]

Another year in which the president's standing with the public was a central factor was of course 1974. The *Times* reported in February that "Republican leaders have begun to confront publicly a crucial question: how to win in 1974 and 1976 despite President Nixon's precipitous decline in popularity."[15] The Republicans' question for 1974 quickly became how not to lose so badly, and their answer was principally to separate themselves from Nixon and emphasize their own integrity.[16]

Politicians and journalists rely on more than bare economic indicators and presidential popularity ratings. Other signs are available. In some years, the Gallup poll spoke directly to the issue of congressional elections by soliciting voting preferences early in the election year. At each election the reported polls are regularly cited as significant straws in the wind. Democratic successes in 1954, for example, were foreshadowed by a shift in the percentage of respondents favoring a Democratic congressional victory from 47 percent in July 1953 to 52 percent in February 1954.[17] In 1958 Democratic support rose from 53 percent in October 1957 to 56 percent in February 1958; this was, it was noticed, "the lowest point the [Republican] party has reached in popular favor since 1936.[18] And in 1974, Republican depression deepened as the reported voting intentions showed their party once again in the worst shape since 1936.

A more concrete, and so perhaps more convincing, indicator of political tides is the occasional special election to fill vacant House seats. The *Times* reported Republicans in 1946 celebrating as a "straw in the wind" their capture in May of a district in Pennsylvania that had been held by a Democrat even though the Democratic candidate was the former incumbent's widow and the party enjoyed a 7,000 voter advantage in registration.[19] A great deal of attention was given to the six special elections held early in 1974. All six seats had been won by Republicans in 1972 with between 52.1 and 73.9 percent of the vote; Democrats won five including Vice President Ford's seat. "Rep. Phillip Burton (D. Calif.) asserted that if the pattern of the Michigan election held, there would be more than 100 Republicans who would not return to the House in January, 1975. House Speaker Carl Albert (D. Okla.) said the results 'mean the Democrats are going to sweep the nation this year.' "[20]

Signs and portents are readily available, widely noted, and generally believed, and so inform strategic choices. Speculation about the party's November prospects starts early. Polls, by-elections, economic news, and other, more intuitive, political soundings are combined to build expectations about the political future which serve to measure opportunity and risk and thus to guide career decisions and political strategies. Imperfect as any of these omens may be, they become, in the absence of better information, important to the strategies of candidates and their potential supporters.

STRATEGIC RESPONSES: GOING WITH THE FLOW

Republican and Democratic responses to the exceptionally strong and decisively unidirectional spring indicators in 1974 provide the clearest examples of strategic behavior. Republican leaders found it nearly impossible in many districts to recruit good candidates to challenge Democratic incumbents, while

Democrats fielded an unusually formidable group of challengers. Republican National Chairman George Bush was in the
embarrassing position of having to explain why, if he claimed
to be optimistic despite Watergate, he had refused to run for
governor of Texas in 1974. "As attractive as George is," a party
official said, "guys are going to look at him and say, 'You weren't
willing to run—what makes you think I should?' "[21] The chairman of the Republican party in Georgia reported that the "biggest problem was candidate recruitment. We couldn't get the
enthusiasm built up. Our county chairmen would just sit on
their hands."[22] He argued that Watergate led people to expect a
bad Republican year and they refused to extend themselves in
a losing cause.[23]

Republican troubles were taken as Democratic opportunities. Linda Fowler, who interviewed all of the New York House
candidates in 1974, reported that "more than one Democrat in
1974 believed he could capitalize on the Watergate scandal . . .
and several echoed the sentiments expressed by this candidate:
'I chose this year because I thought I could win. . . . With Watergate and the things —— was saying, I thought this year would
be a good time.' "[24]

This anecdotal evidence is entirely consistent with the idea
that the relative quality of the parties' candidates is a function
of spring electoral prospects; the relationship posited in figure
3.1 seems to hold. Summary data on congressional candidates
are even more persuasive. Our discussion of the opportunity
structure suggests that the quality of candidates can be measured by their prior officeholding experience. The base office
itself is an important resource. Intuitively, we assume that
people who previously managed to get elected to public office
at least once should be more effective campaigners than those
who have not. They have some experience of (successful) campaigning and wider opportunities for developing skills, contacts, and insights. The evidence in table 3.1, although crude, is
quite consistent with this assumption. In every election from
1972 through 1978, challengers who had held elective office did
distinctly better on election day than did those who had not.[25]

TABLE 3.1   Average Vote Received by House Challengers, by Electoral Office Experience, 1972–1978 (in percentages)

	Democrats		Republicans	
	Prior Elective Office			
Year	yes	no	yes	no
1972	39.6	33.7	39.7	32.4
1974	45.9	41.6	37.1	27.6
1976	39.3	35.0	40.1	31.5
1978	39.8	32.2	43.9	32.4

By the standard of prior officeholding, Democrats clearly fielded an unusually large and Republicans an unusually small proportion of strong challengers in 1974. In table 3.2, the largest percentage of experienced Democratic challengers and the smallest percentage of experienced Republican challengers are found for the 1974 election. An additional figure, the percentage of experienced candidates divided by the percentage of seats held by their party in state legislatures at the time of the election, is also included. This adjusts the proportion of "good" candidates to the size of the available pool of such candidates (roughly measured by seats held in legislatures; no other clearly comparable data are published).[26] The need for this is apparent from the table. The proportion of experienced Republicans is relatively low in 1976 and 1978 even though no strong national tide seemed to be running against Republicans in these years. With this simple adjustment for the size of the pool of experienced Republicans, the difference between these two years and 1972 disappears.

More than 38 percent of the Democratic challengers but fewer than 13 percent of the Republican challengers in 1974 had ever held elective office. More than 30 percent of these Democrats, but only 7 percent of the Republicans, were in office at the time of the election. Clearly, assessments of the political climate had an important effect on career decisions at this level.

Notice that another strategic factor—one largely, but by no means entirely, local—also has a powerful influence on the

TABLE 3.2 Nonincumbent House Candidates with Experience
in Elective Office, 1972–1978 (in percentages)

	Democrats		Republicans	
	%	pool ratio[a]	%	pool ratio[a]
Challengers				
1972	21.5	.36	21.7	.55
1974	38.3	.64	12.6	.31
1976	29.5	.43	16.9	.53
1978	25.4	.37	16.2	.51
Candidates for open seats				
1972	41.4	.68	51.7	1.30
1974	54.7	.91	49.1	1.22
1976	60.0	.88	59.0	1.84
1978	50.0	.73	44.2	1.39

[a]Ratio of the percentage of candidates who have held elective office to
the percentage of seats won by their party in state legislatures two years
earlier.

quality of House candidates. Experienced candidates are much
more likely to be found in races for open seats, regardless of the
election year. This was true even of Republicans in 1974. The
explanation is obvious. Incumbency has such a crucial effect on
the opportunity to move up to a House seat that its absence
inspires good candidates to enter the contest regardless of other,
perhaps less hopeful, signs. This is not an entirely local phenomenon because decisions by incumbents to retire, opening
up the "open seats," are, as we shall see in chapter 5, also influenced by national political conditions.

Additional evidence that career decisions were influenced
by national factors in 1974 is apparent at the level of competition for nominations in the primaries. Fowler reports that
among Republicans she interviewed "the feeling that there
would be a substantial backlash made it much easier for several
candidates to obtain the nomination. In the districts where the
incumbent retired, several candidates stated that they had not
had to compete in a primary because 'this is going to be a bad

year for Republicans.' Others were asked to run because no one else would do it." [27]

The pattern of competition for nominations in 1974, compared to 1972, 1976, and 1978, indicates that the phenomenon was general. Table 3.3 lists, according to incumbency status, the percentage of Republican and Democratic House candidates who ran in primary elections in these four election years. Notice that, among challengers, the highest percentage of Democrats but the lowest percentage of Republicans had to win a primary to be nominated in 1974. Incumbents were affected less, though a larger percentage of Democrats than usual faced primary challenges in 1974.

As one would expect if politicians operate strategically, competition is much more common for nominations to contest open House seats, regardless of the election year. Primary competition is consistently higher among Democrats in all categories. Although it is tempting to argue that this is another bit of evidence for the strategic politician hypothesis (the dominant party's nominations are in greater demand) it may be more a consequence of intrinsic differences between the two parties. The Democratic party is much more diverse a coalition, especially now that the Republican party's liberal wing has practi-

TABLE 3.3. House Candidates with Contested Primary Elections 1972–1978 (in percentages)

Year and Party	Incumbents	Challengers	Open Seats
1972			
Democrats	39.0	46.1	78.5
Republicans	15.7	37.2	73.4
1974			
Democrats	42.1	66.7	91.1
Republicans	25.6	26.3	80.0
1976			
Democrats	40.8	57.0	95.7
Republicans	13.3	38.5	67.3
1978			
Democrats	39.4	44.3	98.1
Republicans	21.3	36.6	68.0

cally disappeared, and Democrats have historically been more intensely contentious than Republicans.

The principal conclusions reached in this chapter can be summarized briefly. Politicians do act strategically. Their career decisions are influenced by their assessment of a variable political environment. Their choices reflect, among other things, the conventional wisdom that national events and conditions affect individual voting behavior. National phenomena thought to be important are consistently monitored and noted; indicators abound. More and better candidates appear when signs are favorable; worse and fewer when they are unfavorable. Clearly, the choices presented to voters between a pair of particular candidates in the district are not at all independent of national conditions; indeed, they are a function of them. The implications of these facts for understanding the links between national events and individual voter behavior are unmistakable. We forgo spelling them out completely, however, until some evidence about other strategic political actors—those who supply funds for political campaigns—has been presented.

4

Strategic Resources

Potential candidates are not the only strategic political activists whose decisions structure the choices faced by voters in congressional elections. Equally important are the people who control campaign resources—money and other valuable forms of assistance. The level of resources available for a campaign is critically important for congressional challengers and the other nonincumbent candidates for open seats. This is no secret; and one important strategic consideration weighed by rational candidates entertaining thoughts of running for Congress is the availability of money and other kinds of help. In a complementary way, suppliers of campaign resources are attracted to potentially formidable candidates. Their strategies are also strongly affected by estimates of probable electoral success or failure. As a result, the same forces that influence candidates' decisions influence contributors' decisions in a way that reinforces the systematic consequences of their strategic choices. The next three sections develop a theory of how congressional campaign finances serve to reinforce the effects of candidate strategies on choices presented to voters at the district level.

CAMPAIGN CONTRIBUTORS:
MOTIVES AND STRATEGIES

The motives and strategies that underlie campaign contributions[1] are more varied and complex than most theoretical speculations allow,[2] but they can be sorted into three broad categories, with corresponding contribution strategies. The mix of motives and strategies differs among the principal types of contributors—private individuals, interest groups, and parties—but the actual choices of whether to contribute and, if so, to whom, converge sharply. Although contribution decisions may be made on rather different grounds, money from all sources pours into contests that are expected to be close.

The most notorious motive for contributing to campaigns is to buy favors, influence, or access to the winner. Economic interest groups—corporate political-action committees, professional and trade associations, labor unions—are commonly assumed to be motivated by hopes of tangible, if unspecified, payoffs, as are private individuals who donate substantial sums. Their rational strategy is to contribute to candidates who are likely to be in a position to help or harm them. Since electoral odds favor incumbents so heavily, most of this money goes to them. But such contributors also invest in campaigns of nonincumbents who have a reasonable chance of ending up in Congress. They thus give to candidates of both parties, sometimes in the same district.

Contributions intended to curry favor are not made with an eye to electoral utility; the idea is to buy influence, not to affect the outcome. If an incumbent is certain to win, so much the better. This explains the behavioral law that much more of this money is available to incumbents certain to win than to challengers certain to lose. How much any particular incumbent collects depends largely on what he is prepared to solicit and accept.[3]

Broader political or ideological aims are typical of other interest groups and of political parties. The rational strategy of groups and parties that desire to maximize their ideological or partisan cohort in Congress is to contribute to preferred candidates in close elections where the marginal effects of the contribution are most likely to influence the outcome. The AFL-CIO, for example, invests most of its campaign money and other campaign resources—which can be formidable—in campaigns of Democrats, incumbents and nonincumbents alike, who share at least some of labor's policy preferences and who find themselves in close contests. Conservative ideological groups have contributed most heavily to nonincumbent candidates with the requisite ideological credentials whose chances look promising,[4] but they also support conservative incumbents who face serious challenges. One company's explanation of its political action committee's policy on targeting contributions described this strategy succinctly: "Target races are those regarded as most important to the interests of the company and our employees. They involve the replacement of a business-oriented incumbent who is retiring, the defeat of a legislator hostile to business views and vulnerable to a strong challenger, or support of a favorable incumbent facing a difficult reelection fight."[5]

It might be expected that political parties would follow a strategy aimed at maximizing the party cohort in Congress, and to some extent they do. But this tendency is weakened by the fact that a good deal of party money is controlled by incumbent members of Congress, who find the congressional campaign committees a relatively painless source of funds for themselves and are unwilling to forgo their share in order to pursue the collective interests of the party. In recent years, the national Republican committees have raised money much more effectively than their Democratic counterparts and have, since 1976, paid somewhat more attention to challengers and candidates for open seats.

Despite some bias toward incumbents, the parties do support candidates according to how close the election is anticipated to be. Past election results and current circumstances are carefully studied to ascertain which seats are likely to be marginal, and contributions are made accordingly. Although the proportionate amount of money they provide to campaigns is small (5–10 percent, normally), party contributions are a signal to other potential contributors that this is a campaign worthy of funding.

Despite the inordinate amount of attention that is paid to parties and interest groups as sources of funds, the most important suppliers of campaign money are without question private individuals. They donate nearly two-thirds of the money raised and spent in congressional campaigns. Although a few of them might expect personal favors in return for their contribution, the great majority make donations that are so small a proportion of the total that they can hardly expect to buy influence with the candidate. The candidate's victory, therefore, takes on the characteristics of a public good for most individual donors. They stand to benefit whether or not they pay any of the cost, and whether or not they actually contribute can have no perceptible effect on the outcome. Thus their motives for giving must center on psychological rewards, which depend on such things as the attractiveness of the candidate, ideological predilections, partisan loyalty, and a sense of citizen duty. Or an acquaintance simply asks for the contribution and it is easier to comply than to refuse. But even these noninstrumental rewards are more gratifying when the donor can be convinced that the outcome is in doubt and that others are also making contributions.

Although objectively any individual contribution has no perceptible effect on the outcome, the individual sense of satisfaction from making it—from doing one's share—is stronger if there is some faith that, at least when aggregated with other contributions, money might help determine who wins or loses. People inspired by partisanship or ideology usually have more than one representative of the cause to choose from; it makes sense to contribute to the tightest races where others are also likely to contribute and where the money is most likely to make some difference. It is also harder to turn down a request for a contribution without the excuse that the candidacy is hopeless.

Divergent motives, then, lead to behavior which is highly convergent. Contributors of all kinds follow strategies that put more money into campaigns expected to be close. This is not mere speculation; the data collected since 1972 on contributions to congressional campaigns confirm that much more money is given to campaigns when there are indications that the contest is likely to be close.[6] The relationship is strongest for contributions to nonincumbents. A fundamental consideration is whether or not the nonincumbent is running against an incumbent; candidates for open seats typically raise the most money of all because open seats are assumed—quite correctly[7]—to be most competitive. But contributions to challengers are also greatly affected by electoral expectations. With minor modifications (interest group contributions to incumbents are, as we would predict, less sensitive to the level of expected competition), the same pattern holds for contributions from all sources.

NATIONAL CONDITIONS AND CAMPAIGN CONTRIBUTIONS

Among the things influencing contributors' judgments about which contests are likely to be close and therefore worthy of investment are their perceptions of short-term partisan political forces. They, no less than potential candidates, accept the conventional wisdom that national as well as local political conditions affect congressional election prospects. Signs that strong short-term forces favor one party's candidates over the other's result in an aggregate pattern of campaign contributions that arises directly and predictably from normal contribution strategies.

Contributors seeking influence or access will give more than is usual to challengers and other nonincumbents of the favored party because more look like potential winners. Less than usual is contributed to the party's incumbents, not because they are bad investments—the contrary is true—but because the incumbents think they need less and therefore solicit and accept less. Candidates of the disadvantaged party are treated in the opposite way. Nonincumbents have worse electoral prospects and so are less attractive investments. Incumbents facing serious challenges because of contrary national trends solicit and receive more money. Their need enhances the exchange value of the contribution; help in a close race earns more gratitude.

Partisan and ideological contributors also give more money than usual to nonincumbents—particularly challengers—of the right persuasion when their party is favored by national forces and to comparable incumbents when it is not. Organized labor provided unusually large amounts of money to Democratic challengers in 1974, for example; Watergate and a weak economy were expected to give them better than normal chances of defeating Republican incumbents. In 1976, by contrast, labor's strategy was to help freshman Democrats hold on to the seats they had won from Republicans in 1974. Republican strategies were just the opposite. Officials of the Republican National Committee, while making ritual displays of optimism, pursued an openly defensive strategy in 1974. "The first priority is incumbents," said the head of the party's political division in February, "the second is open seats, and the third is challengers."[8] "For challengers," reported the executive director of the party's finance committee, "it is going to be very hard to get seed money this year."[9] And so it was.

The logic behind such a strategy may seem unassailable. Mounting a successful challenge is difficult under the best of circumstances; against a strong national tide, it appears hopeless. Hence contributions to challengers of the disadvantaged party would be wasted. At the same time, the party's incumbents may be hard pressed by experienced, well-financed candidates fielded by the favored party. If the goal is to maximize the party's cohort in Congress, it should obviously be more effective to shore up the campaigns of members already holding office than to try to take seats from the opposition.

From the perspective of the party favored by national trends, the situation is reversed. It looks like an unusually fine opportunity to mount successful challenges. Furthermore, few of the party's incumbents are likely to face serious challenges. Therefore funds that under less auspicious circumstances would be used to protect endangered seats may be redirected into the campaigns of nonincumbents.

When national conditions clearly favor one party at the

expense of the other, then, the former's contributors follow an offensive strategy, the latter's a defensive strategy. The aggregate effects on campaign finances are predictable and clearly evident in table 4.1. Table 4.1 lists the average campaign expenditures reported by House candidates, by party and incumbency status, from 1972 through 1978.[10] In the more normal election years of 1972, 1976, and 1978, incumbent Democrats and Republicans spent, on the average, rather similar amounts of money. Republicans display a tendency to spend somewhat more but in none of these three years is the difference greater than 25 percent. The same is true of Democratic and Republican challengers. The 1974 election is strikingly different. Democratic challengers spent, on the average, nearly three times as much as Republican challengers; they even outspent Democratic incumbents for once. Republican incumbents, in contrast, spent 76 percent more than Democratic incumbents and more than four times as much as Republican challengers. Put another way, in the normal years, Democratic incumbents spent between 57 and 63 percent more than Democratic challengers; in 1974, they spent 22 percent less. Republican incumbents spent between 62 and 90 percent more than Republican challengers in the nor-

TABLE 4.1. Average Campaign Expenditures by Candidates for the U.S. House of Representatives, 1972–1978

Year and Party	Incumbents	Challengers	Open Seats
1972			
Democrats	$49,249	$30,176	$96,762
Republicans	52,263	32,340	91,352
1974			
Democrats	46,331	59,331	103,091
Republicans	81,436	20,744	79,903
1976			
Democrats	79,100	44,646	144,060
Republicans	90,184	55,484	97,687
1978			
Democrats	111,424	70,947	212,671
Republicans	138,765	73,043	193,514

SOURCES: 1972 and 1974, Common Cause; 1976 and 1978, FEC reports.

mal years, 293 percent more in 1974. The pattern could not be clearer. Campaign contributions—and therefore expenditures—were sharply responsive to perceived political trends in 1974.[11]

It is also instructive to compare the campaign spending figures for challengers and open-seat candidates in table 4.1 to the figures in table 3.2 on the proportion of experienced nonincumbents from each party running in these election years. The similarity of patterns is unmistakable, as it must be if both potential contributors and potential candidates respond to the same perceptions of electoral odds. But a further point needing emphasis here is that the patterns are interrelated and mutually reinforcing. The availability of money attracts strong, experienced candidates; good candidates attract contributions.

Contributions also attract contributions. That is, one important criterion used by people who control campaign funds in deciding where to send them is what other contributors are doing. One reason for this is uncertainty; contributors want to fund challengers who have some chance of winning, an outcome that is often not clear. The fact that other groups and individuals are contributing funds to a campaign provides some independent evidence and thus reduces uncertainty.[12] Another is that, under the present limits on the size of campaign contributions ($2,000 from individuals, $10,000 from interest groups), contributors can only expect their donations to be effective if they can be confident that others will be giving to the same campaigns. Coordination is essential.

Potential candidates and their potential supporters thus develop a system of mutually reinforcing expectations and actions. They respond as much to one another as to national and local political circumstances. Their strategic decisions reinforce and augment each other and together structure the voters' choices in ways that can be predicted from short-term national conditions.

When conditions inspire counterposed defensive and offensive strategies by respective partisan congressional elites, the consequences are by no means neutral. The defensive instinct to circle the wagons is self-defeating because of the peculiar way money works in congressional elections.

EFFECTS OF CAMPAIGN SPENDING
IN CONGRESSIONAL ELECTIONS

Among the many important findings concerning congressional campaign finance uncovered in research since the first usable data became available (following the 1972 elections) one discovery clearly stands out: the electoral consequences of campaign spending are strikingly different for incumbents and challengers. Spending by the incumbent has little apparent effect on the outcome. In fact, in simple terms, the incumbent's share of the vote is inversely related to how much is spent on his campaign; the more incumbents spend, the worse they do. The apparent paradox is explained by two things. One is that the challenger's level of spending has a very substantial effect on how well he does in the election. Challengers' expenditures are strongly and positively related to their share of the vote. The other is that incumbents adapt their spending to the strength of the challenge they face. The more the challenger spends, the more the incumbent spends. With the challenger's spending controlled, the incumbent's spending is unrelated to the outcome. *What matters, then, is the amount spent by the challenger.*

One of us (Jacobson) has presented the full evidence for this conclusion in earlier writings,[13] so there is no need to repeat it here. The findings are very consistent; the challenger's level of spending is regularly and strongly related to the outcome of the election even when the challenger's party and district-party strength are taken into account.[14] Only in 1974 is the incumbent's spending significantly related to the vote, and even in that year the marginal effects of the challenger's spending are much greater.

The striking difference between the electoral effects of

spending by challengers and incumbents is easily explained. We noted in chapter 2 that individual voting choices are affected most strongly by knowledge and evaluations of the candidates. Incumbents, it is well known, control a variety of resources that come with the office: staff, the frank, travel allowances, district offices, communications allowances, WATS lines, and many more. They use these resources to conduct what amounts to a permanent campaign for reelection.[15] Campaigning of any kind is subject to diminishing returns. Because incumbents use official resources so extensively between campaigns, the increment of favorable propaganda added by the campaign has no additional effect on how well voters know and like them.

For most nonincumbents, the opposite is true. Most of them are unfamiliar to voters at the outset of the campaign. They have not received the exposure and publicity that members of Congress routinely enjoy. So the attention they are able to acquire through the campaign is crucial to their chances of winning.[16]

The effects of campaign spending are asymmetrical. The vigor of the challenger's campaign is crucial; that of the incumbent makes relatively little difference. This ensures that the defensive strategy arising from the converging expectations of the handicapped party's elites will not begin to offset the offensive strategy developed by candidates and supporters of the favored party. Money and other resources redirected into the campaigns of threatened incumbents are much less effective in generating voter support than the resources redirected into the campaigns of the fortunate challengers. If the marginal effects of campaign spending were the same for incumbents and challengers, offensive and defensive strategies could cancel one another out. They are not, so they do not; the offensive strategy is much more effective.

This does not mean that the defensive strategy is necessarily irrational. Even if contributors were convinced that the marginal returns on campaign spending by incumbents are very small at best, they might still rationally favor incumbents in a bad year. A large investment may generate a small return in terms of votes, but if the contest is very close (as are most contests in which an incumbent is defeated), it may be enough to provide a margin of victory. Conversely, the same large investment in a challenger's campaign may increase his share of the vote much more substantially, but if he is far behind to begin with, the gain goes for nothing. Raising the incumbent's vote from 49 percent to 51 percent is preferable to raising the challenger's vote from 30 percent to 45 percent.

Among both candidates and contributors, then, *expectations about the effects of national trends lead directly to the kind of behavior that would fulfill those expectations.* If it portends to be a difficult year, the party fields less experienced and more poorly financed challengers, and they do just as poorly as expected. The other party produces unusually effective challengers with unusually vigorous campaigns, and they do well, again as expected. The political prophecies are, to an important degree, self-fulfilling. The conventional wisdom leads to its own confirmation and so maintains its conventionality.

Voters, under these circumstances, need not respond to national-level phenomena for the effects of these phenomena to be impressed on aggregate election outcomes. Some of course may act on their assessments of the president or the economy, but it is not essential for many to do so to account for the aggregate connections between presidential evaluations or economic conditions and election results. All voters need do is respond to the choices they are offered at the district level (which they do; see table 2.1). One party then does well and the other poorly, in aggregate, because the first has a substantially greater proportion of formidable candidates and campaigns.

CANDIDATE AND CAMPAIGN SPENDING
EFFECTS IN 1974

How large are the aggregate effects of opposite offensive and defensive strategies? Again using 1974 as the best-documented example, it is possible to estimate the minimum aggregate consequences of candidate and contributor strategies. Democratic challengers won an average of 43.1 percent of the vote, an increase of 6.9 percentage points over 1972. Republican challengers won an average of 28.7 percent, a decrease of 5.4 percentage points from 1972. How much of the difference between the vote percentages of Democratic and Republican challengers is explained by the quality of candidates and the vigor of their campaigns? An answer is provided by comparison of the two regression equations found in table 4.2.[17]

The first equation estimates the effects of the challenger's

TABLE 4.2. Campaign Expenditures, Candidate Experience, and the Partisan Vote Shift for Challengers in the 1974 House Elections

	Regression Coefficient	t Ratio	Beta[a]
Dependent Variable			
Challenger's vote			
(N = 320)			
Independent Variables			
Equation 4.1			
Challanger is a Democrat	13.3	14.63	.57
Strength of challenger's party	.477	9.73	.38
Constant	12.5		
R^2 = .52			
Equation 4.2			
Challenger is a Democrat	9.6	10.96	.41
Strength of challenger's party	.341	7.58	.27
Challenger has held office	1.9	1.96	.07
Challenger's expenditures	.144	9.95	.45
Incumbent's expenditures	−.025	−2.12	−.10
Constant	15.6		
R^2 = .66			

SOURCE: Jacobson, *Money in Congressional Elections*, pp. 38–39, 115.
[a]Standardized regression coefficient.

party on the share of votes won in 1974, controlling for the strength of the challenger's party in the district. The second equation introduces variables for campaign spending by both candidates and our measure of candidate quality into the analysis. The additional variables reduce the difference accounted for strictly by party by 3.8 percentage points. But the additional variables increase the explanatory power of the equation substantially as well. The differences between Republican and Democratic values for the prior office and campaign expenditure variables, combined with their estimated parameters, indicate that they account by themselves for a difference of 4.5 percentage points in the vote for the challenger.

This estimate is on the low side. It does not take into account differences in candidate quality which are not measured by experience in office, and, similarly, it does not include measurements of campaign vitality other than expenditures. If elite strategies work in the way suggested here, these things should operate to reinforce the pattern. But in any case, at least one-third of the aggregate difference between the share of the vote won by Democratic and Republican challengers is directly explained by the candidate and campaign variables.[18]

A CONCLUDING NOTE:
SOME CROSS-SECTIONAL EVIDENCE

The evidence offered so far in this chapter has been highly aggregated. But the effects of decisions by congressional campaign elites are also apparent in district-level data. An excellent example is provided by a reexamination of Gerald C. Wright, Jr.'s study of the fates of Republican members of the House Judiciary Committee, who had been at the highly visible center of the impeachment process that led to Nixon's resignation.[19]

Wright showed that Republican members of the committee who favored impeachment did better in the 1974 elections than the average Republican (compared to a calculated "expected vote"). Only one of the six running for reelection was defeated.

Those who opposed impeachment and supported Nixon did worse than expected in the general election; four of the nine lost. Wright's quite reasonable conclusion is that Republicans loyal to Nixon were punished by constituents who had turned against the president. But analysis of the campaign spending patterns in these contests suggests that this is by no means the whole, or even most important, story.

The Judiciary Committee members who favored impeachment were opposed by Democratic challengers who spent an average of about $53,000, which is less than the mean for all Democratic challengers. The four opponents of impeachment who lost faced challengers spending an average of $113,500; none spent less than $70,000. Their average vote was 7.9 percentage points lower than expected. Democrats challenging the five members who won spent an average of only $22,500; none spent more than $70,000; these Republican incumbents did better than expected. In the absence of well-financed opposition, then, loyalty to Nixon was not translated into defeat at the polls. The intervention of candidates and contributors was necessary for the expected consequences of supporting Nixon to be realized.

Reduced to its simplest terms, the story is that you cannot beat somebody with nobody. A remarkable illustration of this fact is offered by the reelection of Robert Leggett to represent the Fourth District of California in 1976. Although Leggett was a principal subject of the "Koreagate" investigation, he was not considered sufficiently vulnerable to merit serious Republican opposition. By the time it came out that he had fathered two children by an aide, had been supporting two households for years, and had even forged his wife's name on a deed for the second house, the nominations had already been set. His Republican opponent was an obscure, retired state civil servant who thought that the outcome of the election "was mostly up to God"[20] and spent only $10,674 on the campaign. A write-in opponent entered the contest after the scandal broke. The opposition was so weak that Leggett kept his seat for another term. He then retired in the face of certain defeat.

5

Strategic Retirement

If one is to believe the testimony of retiring congressmen, none ever quits out of fear of defeat. One skeptical television-network commentator, reporting a rash of spring retirement announcements, wryly suggested that the desire to spend more time with one's family is the biggest lie in Washington. Stephen Frantzich's study of voluntary departures from the House of Representatives appears to confirm the pundit's observation.[1] Not one of his hour-long interviews with 20 of 1974's 38 congressional retirees turned up political insecurity as a primary motive for retiring. The reasons given range from the suspicious desire to be with family to more plausible claims of old age and poor health:

Primary Reason for Retiring	Number of Interviewees
Age and health	7
Lack of interest or other interest	5
Frustration with job	4
Desire to be with family	4

Every entering congressman must, perforce, leave eventually, and given the remarkable ease with which most win reelection few retirees during any given Congress are likely to be driven from office by the spectre of defeat. It is difficult to believe, however, that vulnerability does not occasionally contribute to retirement decisions, particularly in a year like 1974, when Republicans everywhere were hearing dire prognoses for the fall elections. Senator Goldwater offered the chilling assessment that any Republican who had won the preceding election by less than 60 percent of the vote was in trouble; 37 percent of the Republican congressmen fell into that category.[2] That twice the proportion of Republicans as of Democrats retired from the House in 1974 seems hardly coincidental. Yet Frantzich's interviews turn up none of this. Something about 1974 made family men out of a disproportionate number of Republican congressmen.

Vanity aside, perhaps electoral vulnerability fails to show up as a reported reason for retiring because even when the decision to retire is strategic—that is, involves some risk-benefit calculation—it is only one of a number of considerations. Few incumbents find themselves in the predicament of Congressman Leggett, where a quiet retirement is the only recourse. More often, the possibility of defeat will be a marginal concern—though decisions are frequently made at the margin—more likely to show itself in aggregate retirement rates over time than in individual case histories.

Several hypothetical retirement decisions will illustrate how the threat of defeat might operate. Consider the senior congressman who has advanced as far as possible within the House and for whom the value of continued service has begun to wane. Finding his party in general disfavor nationally and facing a tough campaign, he decides the office is no longer worth the strenuous effort necessary to keep it and he retires. A second incumbent finds himself in much the same situation, but for him it is less the diminished attraction of the office than the risk of an ignominious departure. Facing retirement soon anyway and much preferring to leave gracefully, he avoids potential embarrassment by retiring. A third, less common occurrence—but one which reveals the potential intricacy of the strategic calculus—is the senior minority-party member for whom the value of the office would improve if his party could achieve control of the House. For him the chances of losing may be miniscule; he is more concerned with his party's prospect of becoming the majority party. As political conditions sour and the chances of a committee chairmanship fade, this aging member decides not to wait for the millenium and he too retires.[3] This last example

apparently explains the retirement in January 1980 of Representative Bob Wilson after 28 years in the House. According to a
confidant, Wilson, who was the senior House Republican and
the ranking minority member of the Armed Services Committee, decided to retire after President Carter's surging popularity
in the wake of the Iranian crisis appeared to end any Republican
hopes of winning Congress in November.[4]

In each of these three cases a congressional careerist makes
a strategic decision to retire not because of the certainty of defeat but because the stakes (a tough campaign or political embarrassment) have become unacceptable or the value of the office has eroded.[5] Under these circumstances, electoral conditions
affect more than the probability of winning. Even when the congressman's reelection chances remain good and would not have
discouraged a vigorous campaign years earlier, the reduced
value of the office makes the campaign unacceptably risky and
costly. Understandably, a retiring member explaining his decision is less conscious of the reduced probability of winning
than that continued service is no longer worth the required effort or risk.

By this interpretation, explanations volunteered to Frantzich referring to the frustrations of office, lack of interest in the
job, desire to be with family, and in some cases, perhaps even
age and health, are indications of the diminishing value of the
office and the unacceptable risks run in trying to retain it. That
retiring congressmen do not cite political insecurity does not
mean that it is irrelevant to their decisions, but rather that electoral conditions interact with other more salient considerations. If the electoral environment contributes to retirements
which are not explicitly or even consciously strategic, its effects
will still be apparent in the aggregate; both parties' retirement
rates will systematically reflect the current partisan environment. And once again, strategic career decisions will add to the
problems of the party in general disfavor as its incumbents exit
in greater than normal numbers.

We have argued the case for strategic retirements at some
length because it is not intuitively obvious that secure and con-

tent senior members will behave strategically. Representing safe constituencies serves to insulate senior congressmen from the marginal effects of short-term partisan forces. And contentment with a House career eliminates the risky decision to give up the current office to pursue another. Add to these considerations the fact that age and health frequently necessitate departure without regard to politics, retirements should be among the least strategic career decisions, certainly less so than the choices of upwardly mobile challengers (see table 3.1) or campaign contributors. If retirement trends nonetheless follow short-term partisan conditions, the case for a theory based on strategic politicians is obviously enhanced.

The fundamental claim of our theory is that the quality of candidacies will reflect electorally relevant political conditions. For congressional retirements this means that the bleaker a party's fall election prospects, the greater the number of its incumbents who will opt out. Since one party's threat is the other's promise, Republican and Democratic retirement trends should be inversely correlated with each other, and they should be oppositely related to short-term conditions and the November congressional vote.

These predictions follow straightforwardly from the theory; unfortunately, obtaining the data series necessary to test them is not so simple. Aside from the difficulties of compiling retirement rates for each political party,[6] these data have been subject to a variety of systematic influences and shocks during the twentieth century which have affected both parties similarly and which consequently initially obfuscate any underlying negative relationship between the Republican and Democratic trends. In figure 5.1 we see that, even after eliminating the noncompetitive and therefore strategically less responsive South from the analysis, Democratic and Republican retirements are positively correlated. This mainly reflects the secular decline in retirements as congressional careers became professionalized.[7] Even after detrending the series by employing change scores (i.e., $\Delta R = R_T - R_{T-1}$) and beginning the analysis in 1912 (the first year in which one party's change in its retirement rate

FIGURE 5.1   Democratic and Republican Incumbents Retiring (South excluded), 1846–1980 (in percentages)

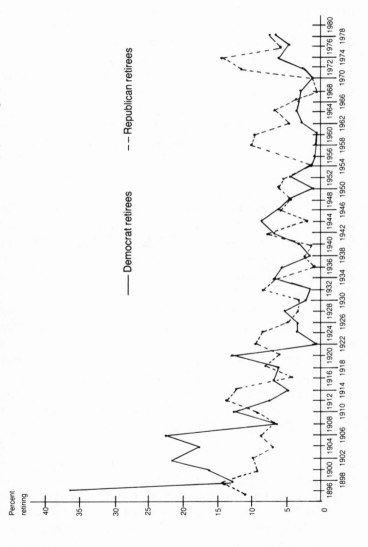

did not exceed 10 percentage points) there remain some conspicuous departures from the expected negative relationship.
Since 1972 retirements have sharply increased within both parties. It is too early to tell whether this represents the transitory,
and predicted, effect of expanded retirement benefits enacted
in 1969 or some new secular trend. Whatever its nature, the
recent rise in retirements runs counter to the twentieth-century
pattern and therefore the years since 1970 will be eliminated
from this analysis.

The second conspicuous outlier is the 1942 election which
also displays more than normal retirements for both parties.
The United States entry into World War II in December 1941
was well timed to shape the career choices of congressmen.
Some resigned early in the election year to accept military com-
missions—although one enlisted as a private—while others
may have moved to government war agencies. The 1942 midterm congressional election has elsewhere been found to have
been atypical in the relationship between the economy and the
vote and, given its special circumstances, this observation has
generally been omitted from time-series analyses of congressional elections.[8] We shall follow this practice.[9]

Removing the secular growth of careerism by examining
change scores and omitting two brief periods which exhibit un-
usual increases in retirement within both parties, we find that
Republican and Democratic retirements do move in opposite
directions. The $-.43$ correlation (significant at .01) of the partisan retirement ratio indicates a pronounced systematic component in behavior which heretofore has been viewed as idiosyncratic. As noted earlier with other strategic behavior, the
cumulative partisan responses to the political environment im-
pose a structure on the vote choices of the electorate. The elections of 1912, 1932, and 1958 are classic cases where everyone
sensed in early spring that the president's party (in these cases
the Republican party) was in deep trouble for the fall congressional elections. As a result Republican retirements went up by
5, 5.5, and 3.5 percentage points respectively, while Democratic

retirements declined by 5, 1.2, and 3 points. Not surprisingly, the Democrats made substantial gains in each election.

The healthy negative correlation between partisan retirements indicates that they are at least marginally strategic. At the same time, the low overall rates of retirement even during adverse periods suggest that the reelection goals of most incumbents are not much affected by short-term forces. Their correlations with economic conditions in table 5.1, for example, exhibit the correct signs but are weak and statistically insignificant. From evidence to be presented in the next chapter, we suspect that, were data on economic conditions for the spring quarter—when retirement decisions are being made—available to replace these yearly averages, the relationships would be stronger. This notwithstanding, the truly idiosyncratic character of many retirements, the resistance of incumbent career plans to short-term political conditions, and the presence of noneconomic partisan forces which also contribute to strategic behavior make these weak relationships neither too surprising nor disappointing.

The low retirement rates also caution us against expecting strategic retirements to play a major role in election outcomes. Even in 1932 only 19 districts were affected by Republican retirements. It is rather surprising, therefore, to discover in table 5.1 that cumulative partisan retirements, whether measured as differences in the change-scores or as a ratio of the overall rates, are significantly correlated with the national congressional vote.[10] We are, of course, explaining change in the vote at the margin; during this period the Republican share of the two-party vote ranged from 41 to 62 percent and no election produced more than an 11 percentage-point shift from the preceding election.

In addition, two other underlying relationships may be contributing to these bivariate correlations. Since strategic retirement decisions respond to the same electoral forces that shape other strategic responses, the retirement rates may be serving as surrogate variables summarizing the effect of other

TABLE 5.1 Correlations of Partisan House Retirements with
the Election-Year Economy and Election Results

	Difference in Δ Scores	Retirement Ratio
	(Δ%D − Δ%R)	(%D/%R)
Economy		
Unemployment	−.07	−.08
Inflation	−.14	−.22
Election		
Vote	—	.20
ΔVote	.36	—
Defeat Ratio	—	.12
(%D / %R)		
Difference in		
defeats	.12	—
(Δ%D − Δ%R)		

Note: The economic variables are the same as those used by Stigler,
with the values multiplied by − 1 during Republican administrations.
Inflation is the percent change in consumer prices since the last election. The ratio indices for retirement (and defeat) are the percent Democratic retired (or defeated) over the percent Republican.

elite decisions with which they are correlated. Moreover, the
causal flow may be partially reversed. The actual vote and the
percent of party colleagues defeated are themselves surrogate
indicators of the "expected" vote during the spring upon which
strategic retirements are based. Each of these explanations is
consistent with our theory. Although with these data it is impossible to sort out precisely their relative merits as explanations of the correlations, an alternative procedure is available to
estimate the direct effect of retirements on the national congressional vote and at the same time to begin to test the mediating
effects of political strategies on the macrorelationships between
the economy and congressional elections.

One of the best predictors of the national congressional
vote is the vote from the preceding election. This autoregressive
feature of congressional elections has been well-documented
although surprisingly few aggregate-level studies have incor-

porated it into their analysis.[11] We suspect that, given political scientists' prior emphasis upon the social psychology of the vote choice rather than its structural determinants, the first explanation offered for its autoregressive behavior would be the glacially changing nature of party identification within the electorate. The results at election T should closely resemble those at T-1 simply because voters have not altered their partisan loyalties much during the two-year interval. But considering the importance of individual candidates in congressional elections—and the ubiquitous effects of incumbency—the candidates themselves provide a dimension of stability from election to election that operates independently of the electorate's partisan disposition.[12] And this dimension is subject to strategic political behavior.

A notorious fact of political life, looming large in this as in every study of congressional contests, is that incumbents make the best candidates. They not only control substantial institutional resources unavailable to challengers, but they are proven vote-getters even before their incumbency. Stated at the aggregate level, a party should enjoy an advantage (or suffer a disadvantage) in direct proportion to its number of congressional incumbents seeking reelection. Electoral victories are subsequently preserved through the incumbency effect, which thus generates an autoregressive relationship. Strategic retirements reflecting short-term partisan conditions alter the structural advantages for a party and accordingly, in the fall, its national vote.

With the relationships provided in table 5.2 we can begin to examine the effects of incumbency and retirement on national congressional election outcomes. Equation 5.1 presents typical estimates of the relationship between the economic variables—unemployment and inflation—and the national congressional vote. Both of the economic indices have a statistically significant impact on the vote and their joint explanatory power argues strongly that congressional elections during the twentieth century have largely turned on the state of the economy. Equation 5.2 incorporates the "autoregressive" vari-

TABLE 5.2. Alternative Models of Congressional Elections

	Regression Coefficient	t Ratio	Beta[a]
Dependent Variable			
National Republican			
Congressional vote (N = 29)			
Independent Variables			
Equation 5.1 (economic voting)			
Republican president	1.84	1.96	.34
Inflation	−28.46	−3.25	−.56
Unemployment	−6.36	−2.79	−.44
Constant	49.34		
Adjusted R^2 = .33			
Equation 5.2 (strategic politicians)			
Republican president	−.66	−.63	−.12
Inflation	−10.00	−1.06	−.20
Unemployment	−8.09	−3.94	−.55
Average vote	.63	2.17	.33
Republican incumbents—			.54
Democratic Incumbents	.04	4.00	
Constant	16.56		
Adjusted R^2 = .55			

[a]Standardized regression coefficient.

ables: the average congressional vote in the preceding eight elections and the difference in the number of incumbents representing the parties in the election.[13]

As expected, the coefficients for both the partisan and the structural variables are statistically significant; their inclusion in the equation improves its overall explanatory power substantially. The betas (standardized regression coefficients) indicate that the incumbency differences between the parties have had a greater effect on the national election results than has the distribution of the previous vote.[14]

One reason why this might be so is that through strategic retirements the incumbency differences fluctuate marginally in response to short-term political conditions. Note that the presence of this variable (along with the normal vote estimate) significantly reduces the relationship between inflation and the congressional vote. Containing a structural, autoregressive component, yet sensitive at the margin to short-term forces, the

distribution of incumbent candidates becomes a powerful pre-
dictor of aggregate election outcomes. We recognize, of course,
that the distribution of incumbents is also connected to the underlying partisan disposition of the voters, so the effects of the
two autoregressive variables are less separable in theory than
these heuristic estimates might suggest. Still, the direct effects
of party differences in the number of incumbents seeking reelection are sufficiently striking to stand as solid evidence for
an important autoregressive incumbency component. The
regression coefficient indicates that a difference of 27 incumbents is worth 1 percent of the vote; this is about the maximum
share of the vote explained in any year by differential retirement.

In summary, aggregate retirement rates during this century
display a pattern entirely consistent with the idea that voluntary congressional departures are, to an important degree, strategic. Democratic and Republican retirement trends are inversely correlated, and their differences are correctly related to
both the election-year economy and the election results. The
statistical relationships are admittedly weak, but, given the nature of congressional retirement decisions, this must be expected. Our structural model suggests that the sheer number of
incumbents a party has seeking reelection (and therefore making decisions to run again or retire) has a significant effect on
aggregate election outcomes. It also begins to test our theory of
strategic politicians against the familiar macroeconomic theories of congressional elections.

6

Midterm Congressional Elections Revisited: A Test of the Theory

Midterm congressional elections provide an interesting testing ground for theories of voting and elections in America. Free from the contamination of national personalities and stylized issues that epitomize presidential campaigns, midterm elections provide a cleaner issue environment for investigating the effects of systematic short-term forces on congressional elections. The seemingly inevitable Eagleton fiascos and *Playboy* interviews give way to more stable—and one might add more important—concerns such as the economy and the government's performance.[1] At the turn of the century James Bryce, in describing American political institutions to his British audience, subscribed to the view that midterm elections provide the citizenry with an opportunity to judge the government:

> the election of every second Congress coincides with that of President; and admirers of the Constitution find in this arrangement another of their favorite "checks," because while it gives the incoming President a Congress presumably, though by no means necessarily, of the same political complexion as his own, it enables the people within two years to express their *approval or disapproval of his conduct by sending up another House of Representatives which may support or oppose the policy he has followed.*[2]

SURGE AND DECLINE

Following Bryce's reasoning, midterm congressional elections would seem to provide an exemplary demonstration of economic voting theory. Yet until recently, the dominant view of midterm elections was much the opposite. If the midterm issue environment is cleaner, it is also more sterile. The absence of presidential contenders barnstorming the country means that midterm elections will generate lower media coverage, lower voter interest, and consequently on election day, lower voter turnout—usually by about 15 percentage points.

According to the "surge-and-decline" theory, under such circumstances the voter returns to the stable cues of party identification and such idiosyncratic local forces as familiarity with the candidates. Rather than Bryce's referendum on the government's policies, surge-and-decline holds midterm elections to be devoid of issue content and meaning. Turnout is lower because voters who are drawn into the electorate only by the excitement of a presidential contest stay home; since these voters are most subject to coattail effects, their withdrawal erases whatever advantage the president's party's congressional candidates enjoyed from his presence on the ticket. Consequently, the president's party should normally lose votes and seats at the midterm. As shown in figure 6.1 there has been an antiadministration drift in the congressional vote for every midterm election since 1938. To the degree that this result is an artifact of the preceding presidential election, the greater the victorious party's surge two years earlier, the greater its decline at the midterm. V. O. Key, who would later defend *The Responsible Electorate*, conceded in 1964 that these "strange consequences lack explanation in any theory that personifies the electorate as a rational god of vengeance and reward."[3]

The surge-and-decline theory contains eminently reasonable hypotheses about voting behavior which, when added up, pose an important dilemma for American democratic politics. Rational, "issue" voting can only occur under conditions of strong stimulation. But within the context of American politics such stimulation is generally associated with the livelier presidential campaigns which are likely to distract citizens from their ongoing concerns.

By treating the midterm congressional election as a mirror

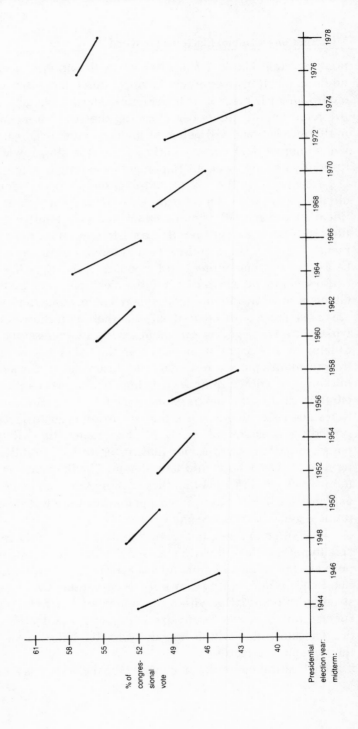

FIGURE 6.1   Two-Party Congressional Vote For Winning Presidential Candidate's Party, 1944–1978 (in percentages)

reflection of the preceding presidential election, however, the surge-and-decline theory fails to recognize some distinctive features of the midterm vote. For one, modern midterm elections have as a set exhibited greater variation in the two-party division of the vote than congressional elections during the presumably more volatile, coattailish presidential elections. Since 1944 the standard deviation in the congressional vote has been 3.9 percentage points at the midterm and only 2.4 points during presidential elections. Moreover, the largest electoral swings over the last 30 years (see figure 6.1) were the midterm elections of 1946, 1958, and 1974. What happened to the jejune political environment, the uninspired electorate, and the return of the vote to some static, normal level?

Moreover, both parties' candidates consistently performed more poorly when their party occupied the White House than when in opposition. The evidence is in table 6.1. Observe the ranking of the Republican midterm vote since 1946. Notice also that within this dominant pattern the congressional vote closely follows the public's evaluation of the president. Unpopular presidents make for unpopular political parties. This last relationship contradicts surge-and-decline and appears to rehabi-

TABLE 6.1. Midterm Elections Ranked by Republican Congressional Vote

Republican Vote (% of total)	Year	Party of President	Presidential Popularity (% approving)
41	1974	Republican	55
43	1958	Republican	56
45	1970	Republican	56
46	1978	Democratic	50
47	1954	Republican	65
48	1962	Democratic	67
49	1966	Democratic	48
50	1950	Democratic	43
55	1946	Democratic	32

SOURCES: *Statistical Abstract of the United States* for years 1967 and 1980 (Washington, D.C.: U.S. Bureau of the Census); *Gallup Opinion Index*, various issues.

litate Lord Bryce. Both the generally poor midterm showing of
the presidential party's congressional candidates and the association of the vote with marginal variations in the president's
popularity agree with the finding reported in chapter 2 that
evaluations of the president's job performance shape some voters' congressional preferences, with negative opinions being
the more important determinant of the vote choice.

With such shortcomings the surge-and-decline view of
midterm elections has been eclipsed by the more fashionable
economic voting theory. But some of the principal observations
of surge-and-decline about midterm voting seem to us to remain
fundamentally correct. Midterm elections are less stimulating,
turnout is dramatically lower, issues are submerged, and the
national forces which appear most effective in generating party
defections are absent. These observations, which are ignored by
the economic voting theory, contribute to the anomaly stated in
chapter 1: a great deal of seemingly "meaningless" voting yields
meaningful election outcomes.

THE ECONOMIC THEORY OF MIDTERM ELECTIONS

Despite the fact that even a casual inspection of congressional
election trends uncovers serious problems for surge-and-decline, it remained the dominant view for nearly 15 years. Then
in 1975 with the publication of Edward Tufte's study the once
traditional, now modern, economic theory of midterm elections
reemerged ascendant. Tufte's analysis is so simple and yet his
findings are so statistically powerful that it has been accepted
and frequently cited as one of the most convincing demonstra-
tions of economic voting theory. It poses a formidable challenge
for better performance to any alternative theory of congressional elections.

Tufte hypothesizes that midterm elections normally turn
on two prominent issues, the state of the economy and the performance of the administration. The first variable is, of course,

a sine qua non of such work while the second follows a substantial literature, beginning at least as early as Bryce, suggesting that the president, as the political system's central and most visible actor, is held responsible for government performance by the citizenry regardless of which political party controls Congress. Moreover, the public's evaluations of the president's job performance are conveniently available through the monthly Gallup surveys. Hypothesizing that the relationships will be linear and additive, Tufte estimates the following equation for eight midterm elections from 1938 to 1970:[4]

Equation 6.1

$$Y_i = B_o + B_1 P_i + B_2(\Delta E_i) + u_i$$

where

Y_i = change in presidential party's congressional vote (V_i) from that party's average vote in the preceding eight congressional elections (N_i). $Y_i = V_i - N_i$.

P_i = percent who approved the president's job performance in September prior to the ith midterm.

ΔE_i = percent change in real disposable personal income per capita from preceding year.

u_i = error term.

Together these two variables explain over 91 percent of the variance in the midterm vote. Moreover, these post hoc estimates better match the actual election results than the Gallup poll predictions based upon preelection surveys. Finally, by serially eliminating observations and reestimating the equation, Tufte demonstrated that despite the small sample size the relationships are not dependent upon the extreme values of any individual election. Clearly, midterm elections during this period have closely tracked changes in real income and presidential popularity.

Despite these impressive results, the economic voting theory is deficient for failing to recognize the prior, independent role of politicians in systematically structuring voters' choices. The sheer statistical power of Tufte's equation does not, after all, preclude the possibility that some other model will better represent the true underlying relationships.[5] Our theory offers a reconciliation of surge-and-decline's indifferent electorate with what Tufte has shown to be highly responsive midterm results. For with strategic politicians responding to anticipated outcomes in the way they do, voters will contribute to national electoral tides by reflecting in their vote the advantages which accrue to one party's candidates as a result of national political conditions. To be persuasive our theory must do more than simply propose a resolution to these contradictory images of midterm elections, however; it must also improve upon economic theory in explaining election outcomes.

Any direct test of the effects of anticipated strategic responses on elections is seriously hampered by poor systematic information on congressional candidacies and campaigns. We presently know little, for example, about the number and characteristics of unsuccessful challengers, the number of congressmen who strategically retire or seek some higher office, or the flow of money into congressional races (at least prior to 1972). Even were good data available, however, the small population of contemporary midterm elections[6] means that we would quickly exhaust the available degrees of freedom. These problems prevent a direct test at this time, but a more circuitous approach is available. Since strategic planning reflects the political environment in the spring prior to the election, measures of political conditions during that period can be used as surrogates for more direct indicators of elite behavior. This permits a simple, comparative test of the strategic politicians and economic voting theories. If the latter is more accurate, events and conditions contemporary with the election should contribute most to election outcomes. Although voters' assessments of the current environment certainly will be weighed against some earlier benchmark, more distant events and conditions are (justifiably) discounted as they fade from memory. The strategic politicians theory, on the other hand, implies that the spring political environment should contribute independently to the fall election results, not through the collective memory of the electorate, but through the choices presented to voters which are established by prior elite commitments. To the degree that elite decisions are more important than economic voting, the spring political environment should be more strongly related to the November vote than the contemporaneous fall conditions.

In order to test this prediction against Tufte's formulation of the economic theory we shall modify his analysis in two ways. First, Tufte uses an "annual" real income series to calculate his index of the economic environment at the time of the election. According to Commerce Department procedures, however, the annual figure is simply the real income level as of July 1. This does not provide the most proximate representation of the fall environment. A better series, and one which Tufte himself employs in forecasting the 1974 midterm election from his original estimates, is third-quarter real income (July, August, and September). We shall use third-quarter rather than July 1 figures, since they also better differentiate the fall from the spring economy as measured by the first-quarter income level.

The second alteration of Tufte's analysis is the addition of the 1974 and 1978 midterm elections and the deletion of 1938. For the latter election neither Roosevelt's spring popularity nor the quarterly income data (in 1972 constant dollars) are available.[7] Omission of 1938 should not be consequential for the overall relationships since Tufte discovered that the estimates were robust against deletion of individual cases.

The other changes in Tufte's analysis do affect the results, however, since the revised estimates in equation 6.1 of table 6.2 are much weaker than those found by Tufte and presented above. The president's fall popularity and the change in real income remain significantly correlated with the vote, but the overall explanatory power of these variables is reduced from 91 to 65 percent. The coefficient estimated from third quarter income data is substantially weaker than the one estimated from summer income data. The economic voting theory is at a loss to explain why this should be. Not so our strategic politicians

TABLE 6.2. Alternative Theories of Midterm Elections

	Regression Coefficient	t Ratio	Beta[a]
Dependent Variable			
Standardized midterm vote loss			
by president's party (N = 9)			
Independent Variables			
Equation 6.1 (Tufte, revised)			
% Change in income, fall	.521	3.30	.69
Fall popularity	.125	2.36	.49
Constant	−9.75		
Adjusted R² = .65			
Equation 6.2 (strategic politicians)			
% Change in income, spring	.691	4.31	.80
Spring popularity	.065	1.82	.34
Constant	−7.30		
Adjusted R² = .72			
Equation 6.3 (combined model)			
% Change in income, fall	.001	.00	.00
% Change in income, spring	.678	2.54	.79
Fall popularity	.099	2.02	.39
Spring popularity	.028	.64	.14
Constant	−10.53		
Adjusted R² = .81			

[a]Standardized regression coefficient.

theory, which holds that the political environment prior to the campaign season may have a strong, if indirect, effect on election results.[8]

Regression equation 6.2 of table 6.2 presents strong evidence for the counterintuitive prediction that the more distant spring political environment will have a greater effect on the election. The overall explanatory power of the president's spring popularity (measured as the average approval rating for March, April, and May) and the first-quarter-based income variables together are substantially greater than their corresponding fall variables. The special importance of the spring setting for the fall election can be better appreciated by comparing the spring estimates with those of even earlier political seasons. In table 6.3 the analysis has been extended to include the third and fourth quarter political settings of the previous year. Nei-

TABLE 6.3. Relationship of Political "Seasons" to the Midterm Vote

	Year Preceding Election		Election Year	
Income base	3d quarter	4th quarter	1st quarter March-to-May	3d quarter
President's popularity	September	December	average	September
Adjusted R^2	−.01	−.07	.72	.65
Significance (F-test)	N.S.	N.S.	.01	.01

ther of these earlier "seasons" is related to the midterm vote. But once into the new year, officeholders and aspirants begin making decisions about pursuing their electoral ambitions, soliciting commitments and endorsements in hope of heading off potential opponents, and looking around for money and organizational support. To the degree that their choices and success in securing support are at least partly governed by evaluations of the current political environment, their actions are represented by equation 6.2. The strategic politicians theory explains not only why the spring setting should be vital to fall elections but also why earlier—adjacent, but premature—settings should not.

The findings to this point provide strong circumstantial evidence that the strategic behavior of elites has a greater impact on election outcomes than do voters' reactions to the economy or the president on election day. A more direct test of their relative effects is accomplished by entering both sets of variables into the same regression equation. Without such a comparison it remains unclear, for example, whether the fall relationships explain unique variance in the vote or are simply attenuated echoes of the spring relationships produced by the autoregressive character of the independent variables. The results of the test appear in equation 6.3 of table 6.2. The high collinearity among the entries and the loss of two additional degrees of freedom caution against overinterpretation of the results. Frankly, given such unfavorable conditions the regression coefficients are surprisingly interpretable and suggestive. All have the correct, positive sign and three are statistically significant. Comparing the standardized regression coefficients, spring real income appears to be the most important variable, but the fall political environment—especially the president's September approval rating—continues to contribute independently to the midterm vote.

The importance of spring income and fall popularity is understandable in light of the behavior of elites and voters. Elites use the current political climate to forecast and therefore anticipate fall political conditions. Between the economy and presidential popularity the former should be a more reliable indicator of its fall counterpart. Because the president's public standing reflects evaluations on many issues some of which can appear quite suddenly upon the political landscape, the president's spring support may bear little relation to his fall popularity. The OPEC boycott notwithstanding, the economy by comparison is generally subject to fewer dramatic, short-term disruptions and should therefore change more sluggishly. This is borne out by the correlations of the spring with the fall variables in our analysis. The cross-seasonal correlation is .80 for real income and a weaker .55 for the president's popularity. Spring income may be strongly related to the vote in equation 6.3 because it better serves the predictive needs of politicians.[9]

While politicians must anticipate the political environment, voters must evaluate it, and for this somewhat different task judgments of the president's performance may be especially attractive. The president dominates the public's perceptions of the government, and as such he serves as an important referent for interpreting politics. Only about half of the citizenry know for sure which party controls Congress, for example, but more than half think they know because many simply assume that it is the president's party.[10] Various recent studies of presidential popularity have found the ebb and flow of the president's public support to be associated with the economy, the presence of international conflict, and other prominent political events and conditions.[11] Evaluations of the president probably link the citizens' satisfaction or dissatisfaction with the politically relevant environment to partisan vote preferences. If presidential evaluations do indeed mediate the environment, this would explain why the president's fall popularity rating is more important than the fall economy in explaining midterm results. Moreover, the greater strength of the fall popularity variable in our analysis coincides with evidence from many of the microlevel studies that presidential evaluations do, on occasion, influence individual voting decisions.

These relationships portray an image of midterm elections which is highly compatible with our theory. Politicians anticipating the effects of economic conditions on the November vote make strategic decisions which structure the choices offered to voters; even voters untouched by national events and conditions can thus contribute to national tides by responding to strictly local, seemingly idiosyncratic cues. The consequence is a strong connection between spring income and the vote even when fall economic conditions are controlled. Other voters make their choices, in part, on judgments of the president's job performance, the net results of which are described in the macrorelationships between fall presidential popularity and the vote. The presence of such "rational" voters who respond to national-level concerns confirms the strategic wisdom of politicians. Together they produce the meaningful pattern of election outcomes.[12]

Strategic Politicians in 1980

Ronald Reagan's victory in the 1980 presidential election was not unanticipated, but few expected his margin of victory to be so large, and fewer still expected the Republicans to take over the Senate. Final preelection estimates projected a Republican gain of at least a few Senate seats, but not nearly so many as to overcome the Democrats' 59–41 lead. Republicans actually won 12 new seats, defeating 9 incumbents in the process, and they now enjoy a 53–47 advantage in the Senate. The Republicans also ran better than expected in the House, winning a net 33 new seats where only 10 to 15 had been projected.[1]

Thoroughly surprised, commentators looking for explanations immediately fell upon the obvious: Democratic congressional candidates were punished for the sins of the Carter administration and their shared responsibility for the twin evils of high inflation and high unemployment. Some even professed to see a thoroughgoing repudiation of all Democratic policies since the New Deal and even a major realignment of the electorate, though this was clearly a minority view. But the theory we have developed to understand how national forces affect individual congressional voters counsels skepticism. A more careful look at what happened in 1980, guided by the theory, is in order.

WHAT HAPPENED AND WHO WON?

A theory of strategic politicians suggests that we begin by asking *which* Republicans defeated Democratic incumbents. One im-

72

mediately obvious answer is Senate candidates; the discrepancy between House and Senate election results stands out clearly. We have thus far focused almost exclusively on House elections, for so does the body of work this book is meant to illuminate. But Senate elections can also be understood in terms of a theory of strategic politicians. They differ most obviously from House elections in being much more competitive; incumbent senators have usually had a distinctly more difficult time winning reelection, and they are more likely to have close contests when they do win. Aside from the clear structural differences between most House and Senate constituencies and other institutional differences,[2] the basic reason Senate elections are more competitive, and incumbent senators less secure, is that they attract a much larger proportion of experienced, attractive, and well-funded challengers.

During the 1970s, about two-thirds of nonincumbent Senate candidates (and challengers do not differ in this respect from candidates for open Senate seats) had previously held elective office, many of them in the House. Those who had not were often prominent in other ways: astronauts, millionaires, United Nations ambassadors, basketball stars. Strong candidates are attracted by the greater status and influence the Senate confers and by a reasonable chance of winning. Contributors are also attracted to Senate races, for many of the same considerations: more competition, the greater power of individual senators, the greater saliency of Senate campaigns. Consequently, even allowing for differences in constituencies, Senate challengers are typically much better funded than House challengers.[3] Not surprisingly, surveys find voters to be more familiar with, more favorably disposed toward, and therefore more likely to vote for Senate than for House challengers.[4]

Differences between House and Senate elections were especially pronounced in 1980. Twelve of the 22 incumbent Democratic senators were defeated, three in primaries, while at the same time, only one of the seven Republican incumbents lost (to a fellow Republican in the primary). Not in recent memory had such a small share (45 percent) of Democratic incumbents won reelection. On the House side the results were rather different. Twenty-seven Democratic incumbents were beaten (two of whom were incumbents in name only, having first won in spring by-elections), but they represent only 11 percent of those running. All but three of the Republican incumbents won in the general election, for a 98 percent success rate. Clearly, Republicans did quite well in both sets of elections, and Reagan's landslide must have helped. But why they performed so much better in Senate than in House races cannot easily be explained by presidential coattails or other national forces. The explanation lies, rather, in the strategic decisions of candidates and those who supported them.

Consider the nine successful Republican Senate challengers. Four were current members of the House and a fifth had been until two years earlier. Two more had held statewide office as attorney general. Another was a state party chairman. The only newcomer was blessed with enormous amounts of money as were, according to preliminary data, all but one or two of the others.[5]

Most of the ten incumbent Democrats who held onto their seats faced much less formidable opposition. One was unopposed, and five faced challengers who were written off early by their own party organizations.[6] In the four races that can be compared with 1974, these Democrats actually increased their share of the vote by an average of 3.2 percentage points. The other four managed to win against substantial challenges with an average loss of 10.3 percentage points in their vote from 1974. Even in the Senate, then, the shift to the Republicans was not uniform, but rather depended heavily on the attractiveness of the challengers and the strength of their campaigns.

The same is true in the House, where, according to the preliminary evidence now available, Republicans mounted substantially fewer formidable challenges. No explanation of House elections relying on national forces is very helpful when we find that no fewer than 73 of the 185 Democratic House incumbents who faced Republican opposition in both 1978 and 1980 actually improved on their 1978 vote. The average gain for

Republican challengers between 1978 and 1980 amounted to only 2.4 percentage points. Republican incumbents did somewhat better, gaining an average of 4.2 percentage points over 1978; 86 of 115 improved their electoral performance in 1980. In both cases, the variance in the change between elections remained high, indicating that local considerations continue to play their predominant role.[7]

A closer look at the winning Republican challengers indicates that success was critically dependent on the quality of the candidates and the availibility of campaign resources. The relationships reported in table 7.1 make it plain that the Republicans did not simply ride a favorable tide. The table gives the percentage of winning Republican challengers according to two variables: whether or not the seat was marginal and whether or not a strong candidate emerged as the challenger. Marginal seats are defined as those which the Democratic incumbent won in 1978 with less than 60 percent of the two-party vote. Strong candidacies are defined as those involving challengers who had

TABLE 7.1. Successful Republican Challengers, 1980 (in percentages)

Republican challenger	Democratic Incumbent		
	Marginal	Nonmarginal	Total
Strong candidacy	24.3	46.2	33.3
	(37)[a]	(26)	(63)
Weak candidacy	3.8	2.5	2.8
	(26)	(118)	(144)

SOURCES: Data on political experience: "The Outlook," C. Q. *Weekly Report* 8 (11 October 1980): 2986–3086; campaign finance data: Federal Election Commission, *FEC Reports on Financial Activity 1979–1980,* Interim Report No. 8: U.S. Senate and House Campaigns (Washington, D.C., October 1980).
NOTE: Marginal seats are those in which the Democratic incumbent won less than 60 percent of the two-party vote in 1978. Strong candidacies are those of challengers who have held elective office or who raised at least $75,000 by 12 September 1980. The table excludes the two challengers who defeated Democratic incumbents who had recently been elected in spring by-elections.
[a]Number of cases from which percentages were calculated.

previously won elective office or who were reported to have raised at least $75,000 by mid-September, almost two months before the election.[8]

Clearly, the strength of the challenger's candidacy is the crucial variable. One-third of the strong candidacies were successful. Only 2.8 percent of the others unseated incumbents, and in two of the four cases involved, the incumbent was under indictment in the Abscam scandal.[9] Marginal incumbents did attract more formidable challenges (59 percent, compared to 18 percent for nonmarginal incumbents); aggregate strategic rationality is again in evidence. But formidable challengers actually did better in *nonmarginal* districts.[10]

Even more strikingly, only one of the Republican challengers in marginal districts who was neither experienced nor managed to raise a substantial kitty early in the campaign was elected. And he was close to the cutoff point, with $69,000 raised by September 12.

Not every strong Republican challenge succeeded, of course. The point is that almost every winning challenge involved a formidable individual campaign which might easily have been effective even without Reagan's victory or Carter's unpopularity. At the very least, successful Republican challengers put themselves in a position to take full advantage of whatever benefits the national campaign and other national forces might bestow, and this was a necessary condition of their success.

STRATEGIC DECISIONS IN 1980

The choices faced by voters in 1980 depended on the strategic decisions taken by congressional activists many months before the election. Our theory argues that these decisions are sensitive to the activists' readings of the political environment. What were the signs saying in 1980 and how did congressional activists react? Why did House and Senate strategies differ so much in aggregate? The data are not yet available to answer all of these questions fully, but enough is certainly known to make a start.

The political omens, while clearly favorable for Republicans, were by no means unmixed. The economy was obviously in bad shape. Double-digit inflation persisted over the year preceeding the election, peaking at 18 percent in March. The administration's efforts to reduce it by cooling the economy only served to increase unemployment. Inflation and the consequent high cost of living were the public's overwhelming choice as the "most important problem" during this period, and these no doubt contributed to dissatisfaction with the administration. Given the close association of the spring and fall economic conditions reported in the previous chapter, Republicans could well believe that the economy would return to haunt Democrats in the fall. But the signals were not entirely clear; Gallup reported a March 1980 poll in which, of those who mentioned a most important problem (with 74 percent specifying inflation/ high cost of living), 32 percent thought the Democrats could do a better job, 28 percent thought the Republicans could, and the rest perceived no difference or expressed no opinion.[11]

Attitudes toward President Carter and expectations about the fall presidential campaign generated even more uncertainty among Republicans. In the summer and early fall of 1979, it appeared that Carter was destined to be a one-term president. With the proportion of the American public approving his performance staying persistently below one-third, Carter was so vulnerable that Senator Edward Kennedy, an unwilling candidate in the past, decided to challenge his renomination. Throughout the summer and fall, Kennedy's task looked easy. Then the Iranians seized American hostages in Tehran and Carter's stock soared. In early December his job performance rating hit 61 percent approving and, with the addition of the Afghanistan invasion, it remained in that neighborhood throughout the critical period of strategic congressional election decisions. Polls which had shown Carter and Reagan running nearly even in September repeatedly reported Carter with leads of 25 to 29 points.[12] Finally, with Carter's resurgence it became still less clear who would be either party's presidential nominee, and this added yet another dimension of uncertainty for potential candidates of both parties. Democrats may lament that Iran contributed to the nomination of the weaker Democratic presidential candidate and, ultimately, to the party's defeat; but Iran may also have limited the damage by holding down the number of strong Republican congressional challenges.

The aggregate indicators of candidate strategies do reveal some movement in the expected (pro-Republican) direction, but it is not nearly so striking as in 1974. Experienced Democrats were slightly more reluctant than usual to challenge Republican incumbents; 23.8 percent had previously been elected to public office, the lowest proportion since 1972 but not much lower than 1978 (see table 3.2). The Republican figure was 20.1 percent, the highest figure since 1972, but no indication of a dramatic upsurge.[13] An unusually large proportion of Republican challengers—about half—had a primary contest for the nomination, suggesting that these nominations were more highly valued than usual (compare the Republican figures in table 3.3). About the same percentage of Democratic challengers had primary competition, a figure at the lower end of the scale for Democrats, but not the lowest in the series. The retiring incumbent Democrats outnumbered Republicans 14 to 2; meanwhile, six Republicans but only three Democrats were seeking higher office.[14]

Other congressional activists—political parties, political action committees, and other suppliers of campaign resources—reacted more decisively. The strategic behavior of these politicians is the most interesting and, for our theory, important aspect of the 1980 election. To an unprecedented degree, those pursuing collective benefits—partisan and ideological—participated in the normally individualistic world of congressional elections politics. While it is premature to parcel out credit for the election results, a close link between their strategies and Republican successes cannot be denied.

These activists are especially important for understanding

the Republican sweep of the Senate. Several sets of decisions converged to generate most of the successful challenges to incumbent Democratic senators. Conservative and single-issue political action committees selected targets from among the sitting Democrats well before the election year and even before it was known who the challengers would be. These groups identified senators they thought were vulnerable for being much more liberal than the voters in their states and they organized local campaigns against them quite independently of any expectations about the presidential election—though not without abiding faith in a long-term conservative trend nationwide. One such ideological group, the National Conservative Political Action Committee, invested in intensive media assaults on targeted Democratic incumbents to soften them up for whomever emerged as the Republican challenger. Others and the national-level Republican party committees joined in, once strong candidates had been recruited, helping to provide the extraordinarily large resource base enjoyed by these and several other promising Republicans.

By the summer, with the economy still doing poorly, with Carter by now well behind in the polls, and with the confidence generated by a harmonious convention, Republicans were following a classical offensive strategy, at least in their Senate campaigns. This is evident from table 7.2, which lists expenditures by national-level party committees for congressional candidates through September 30 (these are the most recent data available). The National Republican Senatorial Committee and the Republican National Committee were clearly favoring challengers and candidates for open seats. At the same time, and with only a small fraction of the money enjoyed by the national Republican committees, the Demcrats were pursuing a defensive strategy, putting most of their money into the campaigns of incumbents.

Other preliminary evidence indicates that the more partisan political action committees also followed sharply divergent contribution strategies depending on whether they preferred Democrats or Republicans. Table 7.3 shows the distribution of

TABLE 7.2. Early Party Spending in the 1980 Congressional Elections

	Receipts	Expenditures	Share Given to:		
			Incumbents	Challengers (in percentages)	Open Seats
Republicans					
National Republican Senatorial Committee	$10,444,980	$3,275,887	7.0	59.8	33.2
National Republican Congressional Committee	11,952,900	1,981,150	60.9	18.8	20.3
Republican National Committee	34,013,904	581,792	13.3	54.5	32.2
Democrats					
Democratic Senatorial Campaign Committee	438,958	363,000	74.8	14.2	11.0
Democratic Congressional Campaign Committee	1,383,211	334,244	59.9	18.9	21.2
Democratic National Committee	6,015,352	374,174	56.8	20.9	22.3

SOURCE: FEC Reports filed from 1 January 1979 through 30 September 1980. The figures for the National Republican Congressional Committee include the period through 30 August 1980 only.

TABLE 7.3. Early Campaign Contributions of Selected Partisan Political Action Committees, 1980

Political Action Committee	Contributions	Share Given to:				
		Republicans	Democrats	Incumbents (in percentages)	Challengers	Open Seats
AFL-CIO COPE	$ 748,920	3.4	96.6	57.1	23.5	19.4
United Auto Workers	1,359,676	1.4	98.6	67.1	17.5	15.4
Business-Industry PAC	129,620	90.2	9.8	24.2	52.7	23.1
Gun Owners of America PAC	122,526	92.8	7.2	9.2	67.1	23.7
National Conservative PAC	128,169	92.3	7.7	19.6	56.7	23.7

SOURCE: FEC Reports filed through 15 October 1980. Figures do not include independent expenditures.

campaign contributions by two strongly pro-Democratic and
three strongly pro-Republican political action committees
(PACs). The pro-Democratic groups favored incumbents; a
spokesman for one of them admitted to a purely defensive
strategy: "Our principal objective was to hold onto embattled
senators and congressmen in marginal situations."[15] The pro-
Republican groups were just as plainly on the offensive: "We
went after open seats and vulnerable incumbents."[16]

Conservative PACs and Republican party committees put
most of their effort into Senate challenges. They did so for various reasons: because they believed that a number of the incumbent Democrats were individually vulnerable; because senators
have more individual power to help or hinder the pursuit of
policy goals; because Senate campaigns provide more publicity
for their cause. Their converging expectations generated candidacies, resources, and campaigns that fulfilled, even surpassed,
their rosiest expectations. In some cases the outcomes were no
doubt influenced by the presidential campaigns and other national forces—at the very least, a disproportionate number of
Democrats stayed home on election day out of disaffection with
the top of their ticket—but the essential ground was laid quite
independently of the presidential campaigns or election-year
circumstances.

House elections were treated rather differently. Here, too,
Republican party committees sought out attractive candidates
and supplied them with some money, information, and special
training in how to run campaigns. And certain Democrats were
targeted for defeat. But the overall effort was noticeably less
extensive, and so were Republican successes. The National Republican Congressional Committee contributions reported in
table 7.2 are indicative; most of the early money was given to
incumbents. A larger portion was almost certainly contributed
to Republican challengers later in the year as it became apparent which ones were mounting respectable campaigns. But
most challengers classified as formidable by the standards in
table 7.1 had to rely on other resources until then.

The exceptions are interesting. Republicans and ideologically congenial PACs had tried, with indifferent success, to undo the Watergate damage in 1976 by going after freshman Democrats who had taken Republican seats in 1974. In 1978 they went after open Democratic seats and did only marginally better. They tried a new tack in 1980, targeting Democratic leaders, committee chairmen, and others who were thought to be vulnerable because their duties in Washington precluded intensive cultivation of their districts and associated them with the national government's failures.

The strategy produced some notable victories; eight of the defeated Democratic incumbents had served 9 or more terms in the House; one was majority whip and five were committee chairmen. Some professed to see this as the result of a $9 million media campaign telling voters to "Vote Republican. For A Change."[17] But, as table 7.1 shows, victories were almost entirely confined to races where strong individual candidates and vigorous campaigns pursued the incumbents. These senior incumbents became vulnerable, it appears, because Republican activists decided that they were and acted accordingly. If our theory is valid, had potential Republican House candidates and contributors anticipated a Republican sweep in the fall, and had they acted on their expectations, Republican gains in the House would have been much greater than they were. The other side of the argument is that even without Reagan's surprisingly strong showing, they would have done well in the congressional elections.

To recapitulate: we do not deny that national forces—the state of the economy, public feelings about the presidential candidates—were at work in the 1980 congressional elections. But a careful look at what actually happened in these elections, so far as it is possible with preliminary information, reveals that the strategies pursued by politicians, in light of their expectations about the likely course of political events, were essential to the results. Individual candidacies once again hold the center stage; few Republican candidates who did not thoroughly prepare the ground were swept into office. Indeed, it is not impossible that the results would have been about the same even if the Reagan campaign had faltered and Carter emerged the winner. The consequences of the 1980 election are sure to be profound; but their causes are not extraordinary.[18]

8

Conclusion: Strategic Politicians and Democracy in America

Electoral politics in the United States is essentially a series of contests between individual office-seekers in which ideas, policies, and parties serve more as vehicles for candidates than vice versa. Although party labels remain ubiquitous, the parties themselves have been reduced to little more than empty structures within which individual political entrepreneurs compete for the "party's" nomination. The few persisting party organizations which take any interest in congressional elections, like the national congressional campaign committees, are usually so penetrated by officeholders that their policies (especially in distributing money) seem little more than extensions of their members' pursuit of private electoral goals. Only in the most recent election, and only among Republicans, have the collective interests of the party been pursued seriously; and here the effort was largely confined to Senate races. In any case, present electoral and campaign finance laws severely limit the parties' electoral influence. Small wonder that within this framework voters generally subordinate their opinions about the economy and the government's performance, even their partisan feelings, to their evaluations of individual candidates in deciding how to cast their votes (see table 2.1).

Since the early days of the profession, political scientists have periodically lamented weak parties and candidate-centered elections and have sometimes offered quixotic proposals for overhauling the party or even the constitutional system. Only if citizens are able to cast informed, issue-oriented votes, they argue, can a democratic polity "learn" through elections. Without a choice between programmatic party teams, how can votes, and hence elections, be meaningful? And yet the aggregate-level research on national conditions and congressional elections reviewed in chapter 2 indicates that congressional elections *are* meaningful. To assess the quality of macrodemocracy it is apparently necessary to understand American politics in terms other than its approximation to the strong-party, parliamentary ideal.

The subordination of issues and the failure of parties to structure choices does not mean that the competition for office is anarchistic. Offices and elections in America constitute a stable political marketplace within which entrepreneurial politicians can pursue long-term investment strategies. The market analogy is apt: the national vote is a function of many private exchange calculations, including those made by candidates and their supporters; the pyramidal stratification of offices emphasizes that scarcity increases value; political resources are distributed unevenly; and a demand-price mechanism operates. This important last feature is described in figure 3.1 in which the "price" (or acceptable risks) of candidacies varies as a function of the probability of winning the election. Candidacies and campaigns in a stable marketplace are predictable and intelligible.

Elite political behavior in America is rational in pursuit of "private" rather than collective—party or ideological—goals. But this does not leave politicians or elections unaffected by broad political issues. On the contrary. Politicians believe that their electoral chances are tied directly to the electorate's responses to national events and conditions. The cumulative strategies of several sets of core actors—incumbents, challengers, and contributors—systematically anticipate the perceived effects of short-term electoral forces. Incumbents nearing retirement consider the difficulty of the upcoming campaign in deciding whether to make another race (chapter 5). Those whose career goals commit them to seek reelection redouble their campaign effort in the face of contrary national tides, but in doing so they draw resources away from their party's nonincumbent candidates (table 4.1). The difference in the marginal effects of campaign resources deployed by incumbents and nonincumbents guarantees that the strategy will be suboptimal from the party's perspective; but it enhances the macrolevel responsiveness of elections to current national conditions.

So too does the behavior of potential campaign contributors. Although their purposes may differ, contributors' strategies similarly reinforce the risk-aversive actions of politicians. The private citizen who is "issue voting" with a check, the ideological organization seeking a more compatible Congress, and the group merely trying to cultivate friendlier congressmen all follow strategies that help the party favored by the current partisan environment (chapter 4).

Citizens may not generally consider national issues in their votes, but elites do in their strategic behavior. The net result is to so structure choices between candidates across the districts that voters observing campaigns and evaluating candidates will, ceteris paribus, come to prefer the candidates whose party enjoys the structural advantages derived from the various elite strategies. In this way congressional elections do reflect the course of American political life. Indeed, models of elections based on elite responses to national conditions better explain marginal variations in the vote than do models that assume direct issue voting (table 5.2 and chapter 6). At present, American congressional elections appear no less responsive to systematic national forces than elections within strong party systems. Strong parties with issue voting is one way to meaningful elections; strategic politicians structuring choices is another.

If these findings suggest that we should be more circumspect in judging the American political system (harshly) against the classic British model, they equally warn us away from that other scholarly pastime of exporting models of American politics across the Atlantic. The British party and constitutional systems minimize the strategic significance of politicians in parliamentary elections in two respects. Candidates are simply less important ingredients in the vote choice than party cues and national issues. And even where they play a minor role in the vote, the strategic decisions that structure the vote choices are controlled, not by the politicians, but by the local and national party organizations.

British parties control sanctions and side payments crucially affecting members' careers and so are in a position to follow campaign strategies—including deployment of candidates and resources—aimed at achieving the party's collective interests. The irony is that, because British voters respond much more strongly to national issues, parties, and leaders than do Americans, the parties can derive relatively little benefit from this capacity. Hence there seems to be less career juggling in Britain than we see in the springtime political jockeying in America.

Consider, more generally, the implications of a strong national-weak local complex of forces versus its opposite configuration on strategic choice and the conduct of elections. In the first case, where the concern with national issues is expressed directly in individual votes, the particular candidates' personalities and promises should be less relevant to the election outcome. In strong party systems this fact discourages the strategic deployment of candidates and resources. But in a weak party market-system, where the numerous, discrete strategic career choices are adapted to expectations about the fall vote, a strong national issue component to the vote will have pronounced effects on career decisions. Where national forces are determinative and the candidate's influence on the vote is consequently weak, the only efficacious decision for a politician in an open market political system is the one that puts him in the right place at the right time. Such a system although thoroughly democratic is not especially conducive to the development of professional, careerist legislators. In many districts congressional careers will routinely be ended by some abrupt perturbation in national political life. Aware of the vicissitudes of elective office and in the absence of the customary side payments strong parties provide, few politicians aspire to the national legislature as a career.

Where, on the other hand, national forces have minimal effect on individual votes but local forces do matter, politicians will be no less strategic, but they will be attentive to a different set of constraints. Structural advantages provided by incumbency and other base offices, and occasional, idiosyncratic local issues such as scandalous behavior by the incumbent, will instead govern the direction and timing of mobility decisions. If the probability of winning is insulated from the external shocks of national political life, career advancement becomes more orderly, even, in the extreme, bureaucratic, in that mobility occurs only with vacancy.[1] Incumbents enjoy the best structural resources for seeking reelection; their prospects for retaining offices are enhanced while their chances of defeating the incumbent in some higher office are diminished. Ambitious politicians must wait their turn as mobility within the office hierarcy increasingly reflects the actuarial tables. Because officeholders here wholly control their destiny, there is ample opportunity for careerism to blossom.

Voters in this scenario are limited to choosing, in most elections, between entrenched incumbents and feeble challengers, with the outcome rarely in doubt. At some point, incumbents become so apparently invincible that challenges are not just feeble, they are not even sincere. The goal of winning the nomination in the primary and challenging the incumbent in the general election to compete for a seat in Congress is displaced in preference to various private goals that are not incompatible with losing. Into the political vacuum rush candidates who use the ballot to advertise themselves or some cause. Young lawyers, insurance salesmen, and real estate agents can all profit from this relatively cheap source of name recognition. Political ideologues and crusaders who have no realistic chance of victory find in the ballot a forum for airing their views. Such occurrences may be applauded in the abstract for giving politically deviant movements access to democratic channels, but they occur at the cost of giving voters real choices.[2]

The logical extension of strategic behavior to these extreme "ideal" types uncovers an important proposition embedded in our theory: *In a market system, the less important candidates and campaigns are to election outcomes, the more closely should strategic career choices follow the national political environment.* When they matter least, strategic choices will be the most responsive to national conditions. And as national forces attenuate so too will career choices based upon them. This is highly portentous for our theory because it identifies the reason why anticipated strategic responses cannot create effects for national forces where no direct relationship exists. The structure of choice can only supplement—not supplant—the real, direct effects of national issues on elections. We have not claimed, and this proposition tells us that we cannot claim, that strategic elite behavior may constitute a stable self-fulfilling prophecy.

To understand the interconnected effects of national electoral forces and anticipated strategic responses on congressional elections consider how these two variables have changed over the last hundred years. There is ample reason to believe that national level forces were more important to congressional voting in the past than they are now. Nineteenth-century party attachments were apparently more pervasive and ardent; split-ticket voting was rarer and presidential coattails were longer. The ticket system bound lower level candidates to the fortunes of their presidential or gubernatorial standard-bearer. The potential candidate's only consequential decision was, in many instances, when and where to run. Politicians were intensely strategic but for elections these strategic considerations did not matter much.

Accustomed to such a system politicians would not necessarily abandon their traditional strategies if district-level phenomena became relatively more important and national forces relatively less so—as they clearly have. Rather, they would by and large continue to respond strategically to national political trends because, *increasingly as a consequence of their own strategic choices*, their expectations about election outcomes continue to be realized.[3] Ultimately, their expectations may come to be based on pure illusion, their prophecies wholly self-fulfilling. Fiorina, speculating about why his research failed to turn up any individual-level evidence of economic voting, closes with an argument similar to the one we make in this book, that "perhaps election returns vary not with objective economic conditions but with self-fulfilling expectations about those conditions held by candidates and parties."[4]

But we do not think this condition has been reached; nor, as stated above, do we think that even if it eventually is, can it constitute anything more than a temporary, transitional state. At present, congressional elites make what might be best described as "self-reinforcing" prophecies. National conditions do continue to contribute directly to voting, so we cannot argue that it is strategically foolish for elites to take them into account. But their strategies contribute a large and important independent component to the national tides.

There is, however, no guarantee that the present balance of national and local forces is stable. Following the erosion of partisanship in the electorate, congressional elections appear to have become progressively detached from national politics over the past two decades. Thomas Mann's figures, reported in table 8.1, are evidence in point. They show the striking increase in the standard deviation of the shift or "swing" in the two-party vote between adjacent congressional elections across congressional districts. The wider variations in the swing indicate a greatly reduced role for cross-district national forces. Comparable data for Britain confirm our expectation that national forces are much more important in that strong party sytem.

Mann's data are consistent with other evidence, familiar to political scientists, that the growing importance of incumbency has reduced the impact of national forces on congressional elections. Even in 1980, 89 percent of the incumbent Democratic congressmen won reelection. But what is known to political scientists will not remain hidden from politicians. Learning does take place. The most educable are the many incumbent congressmen in midcareer who are ideally suited to test the effects of national forces. As we found, they represent the only significant set of actors who are motivated and sufficiently resourceful to combat unfavorable conditions. And political professionals do not lack a framework for revising their ideas about what matters in congressional contests. Even in 1974, with

TABLE 8.1. Distribution of Swing in British and U.S.
Constituencies, Selected Years, 1862–1976

Election	Standard Deviation	Variance
Britain		
1892–1895	3.0	9.0
1959–1964	2.4	5.8
1966–1970	2.6	6.8
United States		
1862–1864[a]	4.7	22.2
1956–1958	5.5	30.3
1958–1960	5.6	31.4
1972–1974	9.6	92.2
1974–1976	9.0	81.0

SOURCE: Thomas E. Mann, *Unsafe at Any Margin: Interpreting Congressional Elections* (Washington, D.C.: American Enterprise Institute for Public Policy Research, 1978), p. 85.
[a]Excludes southern districts.

Watergate and Nixon at the forefront of political speculations, *Congressional Quarterly* reported, almost absentmindedly, that "In the course of nearly 200 interviews done for this [special supplement on the 1974 elections], politicians and local newsmen seldom cited Watergate as the basis of their judgments about who would run well and who would not. They mentioned traditional factors—name recognition, money, organizational contacts, and personality."[5] And the performance of Republican freshmen in 1974 (their average vote actually increased between 1972 and 1974) and Democratic freshmen in 1976 (48 or 49 held onto seats they had taken from Republicans in 1974) has not gone unmarked. Earlier, a typical *Congressional Quarterly* preelection story would be headlined, "Midterm Elections: Bad News for the Party in Power."[6] By 1978 the headline read "Past Trends Indicate Small Democratic Loss," the main explanation being the overwhelming electoral importance of incumbency.[7] President Carter's standing was not expected to make much difference, and it did not.[8]

But even if the influence of national forces on individual voters atrophies to nothing, the coincidence of expectation with result, arising from politicians following outmoded beliefs, should ensure that the national political environment would lose its strategic influence rather slowly. It is not inconceivable that the persistence of current trends—the decay of partisanship, the growing value of incumbency, and the increasing detachment of congressional voting from national politics—could usher in a period of purely self-fulfilling prophecy. But it is inconceivable that this could constitute a stable equilibrium; elites do learn, are learning. The unhappy result might well be the scenario we outlined for a system in which national forces are thought to have little effect on elections. The crucial, if indirect, link between national political conditions and congressional elections provided by strategic politicians would be snapped. Where, then, would we find systemic democratic responsiveness?

Epilogue: Strategy and Choice in 1982

The real world of electoral politics rarely offers clear tests of competing theories. For the election years covered in the first edition of this book, both our theory and the more orthodox economic voting theories predicted the same aggregate results. Only the mechanism was different: Economic conditions and evaluations of the president's performance might operate directly on individual voting decisions or their effects might be mediated through elite strategies, but the outcome would be the same. The alternative theories predict different aggregate outcomes only if congressional elites were to act in ways that countered rather than reinforced electoral prophecies.

This is, remarkably enough, exactly what happened in 1982. Although a great deal of the strategic behavior evident in the 1982 midterm election conformed to customary patterns, some important departures occurred. The most striking and, we will argue, consequential differences were the direct result of the Republican party's newly developed institutional strength. Because national-level Republican committees had the acumen and resources to pursue a strategy aimed at maximizing the party's collective success, its congressional losses were much smaller than should have been expected. Democratic candidates continued to pursue individually rational strategies that, in the end, diminished their party's aggregate gains.

THE 1982 ELECTIONS: WHAT MIGHT HAVE BEEN

Had the 1982 election been a referendum on Reagan and Reaganomics, and had the electorate responded as it has in pre-

vious postwar midterm elections to economic conditions and
its assessment of the president's performance, Republican losses
in the House would have rivaled those of 1958 and 1974. The
economy was in its deepest recession since before the war. By
election day, unemployment exceeded 10 percent, highest in
more than forty years. Businesses were failing at the highest
rate since 1933. The only bright spot for the administration was
the inflation rate, which fell sharply as the recession took hold.
This, and the July tax cut and social security increases, kept
real disposable income from falling, although it did not increase appreciably, either. President Reagan's approval-rating
in the Gallup polls stayed below 50 percent for the entire year;
it stood at 42 percent in the October poll. Only President Truman had a lower preelection rating (32 percent approving in
1946).

Under these conditions, the referendum model of midterm
elections predicts a Republican loss of more than 50 House seats.
Tufte's original equation,[1] updated to cover the period 1946 to
1978, is

standardized vote loss $= -10.37 + .678$ change in real income
(2.46) (.164)
$+ .127$ presidential popularity
(.045)

$N = 9$ $R^2 = .81$ SER $= 1.40$ (standard errors are in parentheses)

This equation estimates the vote percentage, which is easily
converted into an estimate of the number of seats won, for there
is a strong linear relationship between the proportions of votes
and seats won by parties in postwar elections:

percentage of seats
held by Democrats $= -42.5 + 1.9$ percentage of votes won
(.16)$$ by Democrats
$N = 18$ $R^2 = .90$ SER $= 2.09$

The average Republican share of the aggregate two-party
House vote over the past eight elections was 46.2 percent. With
real income unchanged and Reagan's approval-rating at 42 percent, Tufte's equation predicts the Republicans to win 41.2 per-

cent of the vote. This is a drop of more than 7 percentage points from 1980. The seats/votes equation translates it into a loss of about 58 seats, giving them a projected total of 134 House seats for the 98th Congress.[2] Such results would have resembled those of 1974, when Republicans won 41.5 percent of the vote and 144 seats.

The 1982 election was, in fact, nothing like the kind of Republican disaster this model predicts. Republicans won 43.5 percent of the two-party House vote,[3] higher than predicted by about 2.3 percentage points. The result is one that Tufte's equation would have predicted only if, given the state of the economy, Reagan's approval-rating had been at 60 rather than 42 percent or, given Reagan's approval-rating, real income had grown by 3-4 percent rather than remaining unchanged. Democrats actually picked up only 26 seats, less than half the number predicted.

If the 1982 elections were indeed a referendum on Reagan and Reaganomics, voters certainly did not respond to national conditions as they had in previous postwar midterm elections. Neither did congressional elites. The pattern of strategic decisions taken by congressional candidates and those who supply them with campaign resources was unusually complicated in 1982; the strategic choices of candidates and contributors, within and between parties, did not converge as they had in the past. And herein lies an explanation of why the Republicans suffered moderate rather than overwhelming losses.

REPUBLICAN STRATEGIES IN 1982

The system of electoral politics depicted in this book is driven by the strategic choices of individual political entrepreneurs in a decentralized political marketplace. Politicians adapt their behavior to national political conditions and, in doing so, multiply the effect of these conditions on aggregate election results. When a party is expected to have a bad year, the strategic decisions of its candidates and contributors multiply the expected effects. Their individually rational behavior magnifies the collective damage suffered by their party. It is a classic example of the familiar collective goods problem—a problem with institutional solutions. As we pointed out in chapter 3, a strong party might be able to deploy candidates and campaign resources to counteract rather than reinforce the effects of negative national conditions. To an important extent, this is what the Republican party managed to do in 1982.

National-level Republican organizations—the party's National Committee (RNC) and National Senatorial and Congressional Campaign Committees (NRSC and NRCC)—have, over the past decade, gradually become major forces in congressional election politics. One reason is money; Republicans have perfected a direct mail fund-raising system, tapping millions of donors who regularly contribute small amounts of money, that provides them with a steadily growing, predictable income quite independent of fluctuations in the political environment. In 1980, a year of great Republican enthusiasm, national Republican organizations raised $111 million for the campaign. In 1982, with much to dampen Republican spirits, they raised more than $180 million.

Republican strategists have also figured out how to use the money effectively within the structure of regulation established by federal campaign finance legislation.[4] Although direct party contributions to candidates are strictly limited (the law in this respect treats parties like political action committees), parties are allowed to spend additional money on behalf of candidates as part of a coordinated campaign. In 1982, a party could, in various ways, legally put $56,900 into a House campaign and between $91,260 and $1,349,416 into a Senate campaign, depending on the population of the state.

Party officials also had the foresight to use the party's resources to recruit and train high-quality congressional candidates. Much of the recruiting for 1982 took place in 1981. Joe Gaylord, the NRCC's campaign director, said his organization's "main priority" in 1981 was "the identification of good, quali-

fied Republicans" and that they "spent almost all of 1981 car-
rying out that priority."[5] It was, for most of the year, a splendid
time to be recruiting Republican candidates. Reagan's approval-
rating hovered near 60 percent from March through October as
he won major legislative victories with a program that prom-
ised prosperity without inflation. Surveys taken in late spring
showed a significant shift of voters to the Republican column;
an Associated Press–NBC News poll taken in May found Republicans ahead for the first time in almost thirty years on the
question of which party people wanted to win the next
congressional election.[6] Republicans also anticipated gains from
reapportionment, which shifted 17 House seats from the North-
east and Midwest to the presumably more conservative South
and West. Talk was of realignment and perhaps a Republican
House after 1982.

By the fall of 1981, however, these grand hopes began to
fade. The economy slid deeper into recession. Reagan's approval-
rating in the Gallup poll began to sag. By November it had
dropped below 50 percent for the first time. Polls showed voters returning to their traditional Democratic preferences both
in party identification and for congressional candidates. By the
beginning of 1982, the picture for Republicans began to look
bleak indeed.

Republican party officials were understandably worried that
the good candidates they had recruited would be scared off;
"I'd check every day," said Nancy Sinnott, the NRCC's executive director, "but it wasn't happening."[7] Thus the party's early
work paid unexpected dividends. Republican consultant Eddie
Mahe said in March that "we had so many candidates out so
early, we're in pretty good shape. If the heavy decision making
was going on now, we might be suffering" because of the expected impact of the recession. He compared 1982 with 1974,
when Watergate and another recession scared off good Republican candidates: "the candidates we had that year couldn't even
be the drivers for this year's bunch."[8]

Republican recruitment did not, to be sure, survive the

recession unscathed. Three midwestern Republican governors chose not to seek reelection and a fourth declined to challenge a Senate incumbent. The economy was a factor in all of these decisions; all of them weakened the Republican ticket. Late in the spring, a few strong House candidates the party had worked to recruit dropped out, particularly in states in which late redistricting heightened uncertainty (and prevented early commitments).[9] But there was no sign that the damage was widespread, "no evidence of the sort of panicky rededication to the practice of law"[10] observed among potential Republican candidates in 1974.

Republican leaders invested heavily in recruitment because they have become convinced that strong candidates are crucial to their party's overall success. Representative Vander Jagt, chairman of the NRCC, said in February that "just as they say pitching is 80 percent of baseball, in a Congressional race the candidate is 80 percent of winning. A good candidate can win it, no matter how bad the conditions, and a bad candidate can lose it, no matter how good the conditions."[11] He was of course trying to encourage candidates the party had recruited to stay in the race despite disheartening trends, but national party efforts clearly reflected this kind of thinking.

The success of these efforts is evident not only in the comments of Republican officials but also in our simple measure of candidate quality: 24 percent of the Republican challengers in 1982 had previously held elective office.[12] This is a higher proportion of experienced Republican challengers than appeared in 1972 or 1980. They were a significantly more experienced group than would be expected under conditions holding early in the election year;[13] Republican candidates' career-decisions did not, in aggregate, reflect the strategic orientations of the past. This is one important factor distinguishing 1982 from other postwar midterm elections. It cannot, by itself, explain why Republicans' net losses were smaller than expected, for only one Republican challenger (a state senator, to be sure) defeated a Democratic incumbent. But it did affect the strategic decisions of other activists, which ultimately limited Democratic gains.

Why, if Republicans managed to recruit so many good challengers, did only one of them win? Part of the reason is that, although Republican candidates did not adapt their strategic decisions to strongly negative national trends, Republican campaign contributors ultimately did. The director of political education for the Business–Industry PAC (BIPAC), Bernadette Budde, tried to convince contributors that "the economy matters for a party only if its candidates think it matters";[14] they were evidently not persuaded.

For several reasons, business-related PACs, which had generously funded Republican challengers in 1980, turned this time to defending incumbents. For one, the deepening recession and decreasing public support for Reagan and Reaganomics encouraged traditional defensive strategy along the lines described in chapter 4. Given Democratic control of the House, business PACs were especially sensitive to the political breezes; simply stated, they were reluctant to contribute *against* Democratic incumbents with whom they might have to do business as the odds on defeating them appeared to lengthen. "PACs looked at the candidates and concluded by last June that this would not be a year to sacrifice their position with certain incumbents," according to Vincent J. Breglio, the NRSC's executive director.[15]

Moreover, in a sense, their success in 1980 dictated a defensive posture in 1982. Business PAC officials concluded that most of the easy targets among Democratic incumbents had been picked off in 1980; and now they had an unusually large number of freshman Republicans who seemed to be at risk. Thus a strategy of protecting recent gains evolved. "The PACs were so successful in 1980 that they're not taking risks on challengers," noted the editor of a newsletter on PACs during the campaign. "They're focusing on vulnerable freshmen they helped elect two years ago."[16] BIPAC's president, Joseph Fanelli, said his group "was in a hold position. If we can just hold the gains we made in 1980, we'll be doing well."[17] The 1982 Republican challengers were, paradoxically, victims of their party's success in 1980.

Redistricting was given as one more reason for protecting incumbents. Lines drawn late in the election year made it more difficult to choose which challengers' races to target. And, as a PAC spokesman explained it, "some districts have been reshaped so drastically that the incumbent has, in essence, a new district. Incumbents, in effect, will have to run as hard as challengers, and they'll need extra help."[18]

Republican incumbents, worried about voters' possible reactions to the deep recession, naturally encouraged the PACs' defensive disposition. As usual, their own reelection needs took precedence over the collective interests of their party. A nice example is provided by Representative James Hansen of Utah, whose narrowly successful challenge in 1980 had benefited from more than $80,000 in PAC money. His 1982 solicitation letter to PACs urged them to "shift gears in the changing climate." "It is clear," he wrote (quite groundlessly), "that 1982 will not have as many attractive challengers as the last two elections. . . . I would hope that my friends would budget a substantial amount for incumbents," and, more to the point, send $1,000.[19]

Deteriorating economic conditions and the decline in Reagan's approval-ratings eventually pushed Republican party organizations into a defensive stance as well. Although party committees were wealthy enough to support to the legal limit any challenger with a plausible chance of winning, explicit priorities were established for focusing party efforts during the latter stages of the campaign. Freshmen and other potentially vulnerable incumbents were given top priority; next were candidates for open seats; challengers were last in line. Offering common sense as the basic rationale for a defensive posture, the RNC's communications director argued that "more often than not, it's easier to protect what you've got than go after something else."[20] More than a few challengers who had succumbed to the party's blandishments in the heady days of 1981 evidently had reason to regret it.

DEMOCRATIC STRATEGIES IN 1982

Republican *contributors*, then, generally behaved as expected when conditions are unfavorable, but Republican *candidates* did not. Among Democrats a different pattern emerged that, in its own way, was also at variance with the market model advanced in chapter 3. Democratic candidates were of the quality expected when national conditions strongly favor a party; but contributions to Democrats were decidedly more defensive than past patterns of support would lead us to expect. As a result, many of these promising candidacies were inadequately financed and so ultimately came up short.

As it had in previous election years, Democratic recruitment reflected developing national conditions. Representative Tony Coelho, chairman of the Democratic Congressional Campaign Committee, said in March that Democrats had found it hard to attract good candidates during most of 1981 but that things began to improve in the fall. "Now they're coming to me because they smell victory in 1982."[21] Earlier, with recruitment going poorly, he had rationalized that "a national atmosphere, or a regional atmosphere, that is conducive to your party" is more important to electoral success than recruiting strong candidates.[22] But as Democratic recruitment picked up he shifted to the view that "the critical time for the November elections is November through February, when candidates decide to run or not. Whoever has the best candidates usually still wins."[23]

In the end, Democrats fielded an exceptionally attractive group of challengers. About 43 percent of them had previously won election to public office, a very high proportion by historical standards—higher, indeed, than in 1974. Republican freshmen attracted especially strong opposition; nearly 60 percent of their challengers had held elective office, a figure much more typical of candidates for open seats. But, like Republican challengers, many high-quality Democratic challengers found it difficult to raise adequate campaign funds.

One reason was that much of the money available to Democrats was absorbed by incumbents who did not, as things turned out, need it. This is one important way in which Republican fund-raising and recruitment successes paid off. Many Democratic incumbents who might otherwise have expected weak, underfinanced challengers in a year like 1982 had to be prepared for potentially formidable opposition. Memories of the 1980 election, in which a considerable number of apparently "safe" senior Democratic incumbents fell victim to lavishly financed Republican challenges, were still fresh enough to recommend caution. Caution occasionally reached absurd proportions. As of June 30, Stephen Solarz of New York had $657,364 on hand; Charles Schumer of New York reported $480,711; Dan Rostenkowski of Illinois, $396,332.[24] All three of these incumbent Democrats had won by large margins in 1980 (the lowest with 74 percent of the vote); all three won more than 80 percent of the vote in 1982.

Even if strong opposition did not materialize—and Coelho claimed in September that Republican campaigns against incumbent Democrats had definitely "slowed down"[25]—enough uncertainty was created to prevent incumbents from relaxing their fund-raising efforts until well into the campaign. Challengers were thus starved for funds during the crucial summer months. At midsummer, the average Democratic incumbent had raised seven times as much money as the average Democratic challenger.

Democratic fund-raising in 1982 provides a particularly clear illustration of how the individual electoral interests of incumbents can conflict with the collective electoral interests of their party. Each incumbent wants campaign resources distributed in a way that minimizes his or her own risk of defeat. The party is better off, collectively, distributing resources in a way that maximizes its aggregate gains. Rationally, it should redirect resources to nonincumbents up to the point where expected gains match expected losses among incumbents. In the abstract, it does not matter to a party which specific candidates win; what counts is the total number of seats it takes. Individual candidates, on the other hand, care very much who the particular winners are. Given any influence in the matter, incumbents will cultivate a distribution of campaign resources that reduces their own electoral risk even though it diminishes their party's overall success.[26]

Democratic challengers faced another special fund-raising problem. Incumbents, Democrats and Republicans alike, have little difficulty raising money from business-oriented PACs, the most rapidly growing source of campaign funds.[27] The many groups that give to ensure "access" find it wise to invest in their campaigns regardless of partisanship or ideology. Such PACs also contribute, for ideological reasons, to nonincumbent Republicans they think have a shot at winning (and a number of them take cues from Republican party organizations in making their choices). They rarely finance nonincumbent Democrats, who are neither ideologically congenial nor in Congress. This means that, on the Democratic side, business PAC money is not distributed in a way that reflects election year conditions; Democratic challengers are the poorer for it.

Many nonincumbent Democrats did eventually receive significant PAC support, much of it from organized labor but also from newly organized liberal PACs, many focusing on specific issues like women's rights, the environment, and the nuclear freeze.[28] The 22 victorious Democratic challengers raised, on average, more than $96,000 from PACs, about a third of the average $287,600 they raised. But data on campaign contributions through mid-October suggest that labor PACs, which remain the most important source of PAC money for Democrats, were contributing more cautiously than conditions warranted. Table E.1 shows the percentage of labor PAC contributions made to congressional candidates from 1972 through 1982 according to the incumbency status of the candidate. Keep in mind that 95 percent of labor contributions go to Democrats. The distribution of contributions in 1982 is much closer to that of 1976 or 1978 than to that of 1974, the year with conditions most similar to 1982. At the same time, labor PACs were clearly more willing to support nonincumbents in 1982 than they had been in 1980, when their pattern of contributions was decidedly defensive.

TABLE E.1.   Labor PAC Contributions, 1972–1982 (in
              percentages)

Year	Incumbents	Challengers	Open Seats
1972	53	28	19
1974	49	30	23
1976	63	21	16
1978	63	21	16
1980	74	16	11
1982[a]	59	26	15

SOURCE: 1972–80, Joseph E. Cantor, *Political Action Committees: Their Evolution and Growth and Their Implications for the Political System*, Report No. 81-246, Congressional Reference Service, Library of Congress, 6 November 1981, p. 121; 1982, FEC News Release, 7 January 1983.
[a]Through 13 October 1982.

Democratic challengers' financial problems were compounded by their party's relative poverty. Republican House candidates received more than $7.3 million from party sources (including coordinated expenditures), Democrats less than $1 million.[29] The candidacy of Paul Offner, a Wisconsin state senator challenging a Republican elected to his first term in 1980 with 51 percent of the vote, illustrates the problem. "They tell me I'm the party's third-highest priority challenger this year," he said in October. "But if you add up all the money I've gotten from the national committee, from the congressional campaign committee, from the state party, it comes to $1,000."[30] Thus the organizations with the strongest direct concern with encouraging successful Democratic challengers simply lacked the resources to help them take advantage of Republican difficulties.

CASHING IN: THE ELECTION RESULTS

Neither party followed, collectively, a strategy that would have consistently reinforced the electoral effects of the deep recession and unpopular administration. Republicans deployed their centrally controlled resources to counter the effects of bad times, inducing Democrats to operate more defensively than conditions would warrant. The aggregate result was that Republican losses were much smaller than past patterns would lead us to predict. A detailed breakdown of House seats won and lost in 1982 is presented in table E.2. These data show that the Republicans cut their losses by saving threatened incumbents and by almost breaking even in contests for open seats. A comparison with 1974 is instructive; that year, Republicans lost 36 incumbents (32 net) and 13 open seats (11 net).

These results reflect the strategic priorities established by Republican officials as election day approached. During the final weeks of the campaign, Republican committees poured money and technical assistance into those races that their frequent tracking surveys told them would be very close. Nearly all of them involved Republican incumbents or candidates for open seats. The NRCC paid about $2 million in bills for its House candidates in tight contests during this period. The postelection consensus among Democratic and Republican campaign officials was that this work saved the Republicans from 10 to 20 seats.[31]

The logic of investing heavily in open seats is clear; the Republican candidate is not saddled with responsibility for national conditions, and the Democratic candidate does not enjoy the advantages of incumbency. But so is the logic of working to shore up vulnerable incumbents in tight races. As we pointed out in chapter 4, even though the marginal return (in terms of votes) on campaign spending for incumbents is very small relative to that for challengers, a party is better off raising an incumbent's vote from 49 percent to 51 percent than raising a challenger's vote from 30 percent to 45 percent. Furthermore, there is statistical evidence that campaign spending *does* make a difference to incumbent candidates whose party is at a serious disadvantage because of election year conditions. Campaign spending by Republican incumbents in 1974 was positively and significantly related to how well they did in that election; this is the only instance since data on campaign money have been available in which incumbent spending made a statistically significant difference.[32]

TABLE E.2. Results of the 1982 Elections for U.S.
Representative

Type of Race	Won by		Net Republican Change
	Democrat	Republican	
Democratic incumbent vs. Republican challenger	208	1	1
Republican incumbent vs. Democratic challenger	22	140	−22
Democratic incumbent vs. Republican incumbent	4	2	−2
Open seats:			
Formerly Democratic	18	3	3
Formerly Republican	5	10	−5
New	12	10	−1
Total	269	166	−26

SOURCE: *C.Q. Weekly Report* 40 (6 November 1982); 2780–84.

There are reasons to think that campaign money *would* be more important to disadvantaged incumbents in a bad year. In this situation, the campaign is more than simply an extension of the reelection work they have been doing all along. New messages may have to replace old ones. A member who has been celebrating his budget-cutting prowess suddenly has to show he has compassion too. One who has made a point of his support for the administration finds it wise to separate himself from a few of its less popular policies; support for Ronald Reagan is balanced by criticism of James Watt, for example. Money is useful in the battle to define what the contest is about, in trying to cast it as a local rather than national event. The abundant funds available to Republican incumbents in 1982 could indeed be put to good use.

SENATE ELECTIONS IN 1982

As usual, our analysis has focused on the House elections. But the Senate elections, though distinguished by the usual profusion of idiosyncratic factors, are also of some theoretical

interest. Although neither party made a net gain of Senate seats—
the Democrats failed, by this measure, to take advantage of national conditions—patterns of competition in Senate contests
were actually closer than those in House contests to what we
would expect to follow from traditional career and contribution strategies.

Democrats held an unusually large share of the seats up for
election in 1982; 19 Democratic Senators sought reelection; 18
of them were successful. The only loser (Senator Cannon of
Nevada) was brushed by scandal. Although Republican strategists had hoped to fortify their majority in the Senate as insurance for 1984 and 1986, when a disproportionate number of
Republican seats are up, they could not. In a number of states
Republicans had trouble recruiting able candidates; only three
or four of the incumbent Democrats were ultimately challenged
by attractive, well-financed Republicans.

A majority of the 11 Republican incumbents was strongly
challenged, although only one of them was defeated. In 6 other
cases the vote was close; a switch of fewer than 35,000 votes,
properly distributed, would have given the Democrats control
of the Senate. No doubt this would have been interpreted as a
decisive repudiation of Republican leaders and policies.[33] In
all but a couple of these contests the Republican incumbent
enjoyed a very large financial advantage—generally on the order of two-to-one—to help stave off defeat.

CONCLUDING OBSERVATIONS

Our theory of congressional elections offers, we believe, a compelling explanation of why Republican losses in the 1982 midterm congressional election were half what the referendum
model predicted. National political conditions are translated
into aggregate election outcomes through the medium of elite
decisions and strategies. In past elections, these decisions have
reinforced the expected effects of national conditions; in 1982,
in some important respects, they did not. Republicans were the

beneficiaries. Republicans showed how centralized control over abundant resources, shrewdly exploited, can serve a party's collective interests; the Democrats showed how the usual electoral individualism can damage them.

A central argument of this book has been that the quality of candidates is an important electoral variable. Fully 17 of the 23 House incumbents who lost in 1982 were defeated by candidates who had previously held elective office (and this does not count the 6 who lost to other incumbents they faced because of redistricting). A majority of the 81 House freshmen in the class of '82 had served in state legislatures. Republican officials have, in recent years, discovered that state legislators comprise the most promising pool of potential congressional candidates and have worked accordingly to recruit, train, and elect them. These efforts continued in 1982.[34] This suggests that the development of the national party's institutional capacity for effective involvement in congressional election politics has by no means reached its limit. Neither, then, has its capacity to alter the strategic environment of congressional elections.

Notes

CHAPTER 2

1. Raymond Moley, describing the 1946 congressional campaigns in "The Presidency," *Newsweek*, November 11, 1946, p. 116.
2. Richard M. Nixon, *Six Crises* (New York: Doubleday, 1962), p. 310.
3. Gerald H. Kramer, "Short-Term Fluctuations in U.S. Voting Behavior," *American Political Science Review* 65 (1971): 131–43.
4. Some of the best work has in fact been a direct response to some previously published papers: Stigler's replication of Kramer and Arcelus and Meltzer's response to Bloom and Price. See G. J. Stigler, "General Economic Conditions and National Elections," *American Economic Review* 63 (1973): 160–67; Francisco Arcelus and Allan H. Meltzer, "The Effect of Aggregate Economic Variables on Congressional Elections," *American Political Science Review* 69 (1975): 1232–39; Howard S. Bloom and H. Douglas Price, "Voter Response to Short-Run Economic Conditions: The Asymmetric Effect of Prosperity and Recession," *American Political Science Review* 69 (1976): 1240–54.
5. Consider Stigler's equation (ibid., p. 163, no. 11), where he alters Kramer's analysis by (1) changing the time series (1902–70), (2) using the change in the vote rather than the level of the vote and (3) using the change in the economic indices over a two-year period rather than Kramer's yearly scores:

Vote = .49 + .028 (White House Party) − .0084 (Unemployment)
        (t = 2.19)   (t = 1.93)
      − .109 (Real Income) − .326 (Inflation).
      (t = .69)   (t = 3.50)
      R = .38   D.W. = 1.65

6. Edward R. Tufte, "Determinants of the Outcomes of Midterm Congressional Elections," *American Political Science Review* 69 (1975): 812–26; see also his *Political Control of the Economy* (Princeton: Princeton University Press, 1978), chap. 5.
7. Tufte, "Midterm Congressional Elections," p. 826.
8. Anthony Downs, *An Economic Theory of Democracy* (New York: Harper and Row, 1957).
9. Kramer, "U.S. Voting Behavior," p. 134.

10. M. Stephen Weatherford, "Social Class, Economic Condition, and Political Translation: The 1974 Recession and the Vote for Congress" (Paper delivered during the Annual Meeting of the Western Political Science Association, Portland, Ore., March 22–24, 1979), pp. 3–7.

11. Arcelus and Meltzer, "Congressional Elections," p. 1234.

12. See M. Margaret Conway and Mikel L. Wyckoff, "Vote Choice in the 1974 Congressional Elections: A Test of Competing Explanations" (Paper delivered during the Annual Meeting of the Midwest Political Science Association, Chicago, April 21–23, 1977); Arthur H. Miller and Richard Glass, "Economic Dissatisfaction and Electoral Choice" (paper, Center for Political Studies, University of Michigan, 1977); Morris P. Fiorina, "Economic Retrospective Voting in American National Elections: A Micro-Analysis," *American Journal of Political Science* 22 (1978): 426–43; Donald R. Kinder and D. Roderick Kiewiet, "Economic Discontent and Political Behavior: The Role of Personal Grievances and Collective Economic Judgments in Congressional Voting," *American Journal of Political Science* 23 (1979): 495–527; M. Stephen Weatherford, "Economic Conditions and Electoral Outcomes: Class Differences in the Political Response to Recession," *American Journal of Political Science* 22 (1978): 917–38 and "The 1974 Recession and the Vote for Congress."

13. Morris P. Fiorina, "Short and Long-term Effects of Economic Conditions on Individual Voting Decisions," (Paper delivered during the Second International Workshop on the Politics of Inflation, Unemployment, and Growth, Bonn, West Germany, January 4–6, 1979), p. 27.

14. Samuel Kernell, "Presidential Popularity and Negative Voting: An Alternative Explanation of the Midterm Congressional Decline of the President's Party," *American Political Science Review* 71 (1977): 44–66. Other studies have also produced evidence that presidential evaluations affect congressional voters, although in most instances the effects are slight compared to those of other variables. See Robert B. Arseneau and Raymond E. Wolfinger, "Voting Behavior in Congressional Elections," (Paper delivered during the Annual Meeting of the American Political Science Association, New Orleans, September 4–8, 1973); Robert B. Arseneau, "Motivational Conflict and Split Ticket Voting," (Paper delivered during the Annual Meeting of the American Political Science Association, San Francisco, September 2–5, 1975); Candice J. Nelson, "The Effects of Incumbency on Voting in Congressional Elections, 1964–1974," (Paper delivered during the Annual Meeting of the American Political Science Association, Chicago, September 2–5, 1976); Thomas E. Mann and Raymond E. Wolfinger, "Candidates and Parties in Congressional Elections," (Paper delivered during the Annual Meeting of the American Political Science Association, August 31–September 3, 1979).

15. Miller and Glass, "Electoral Choice."

16. M. Margaret Conway and Mikel L. Wyckoff, "Vote Choice in the 1974 Senate Elections" (paper, College Park, Maryland, July 1979) and "Vote Choice in the 1974 Congressional Elections."

17. Miller and Glass, "Electoral Choice," p. 34.

18. Conway and Wyckoff, "Vote Choice in the 1974 Congressional Elections," p. 24 and "Vote Choice in the 1974 Senate Elections," tables 4 and 5.

19. Jack M. McLeod, Jane D. Brown, and Lee B. Becker, "Watergate and the 1974 Congressional Elections," *Public Opinion Quarterly* 41 (1977): 181–95.
20. Kinder and Kiewiet, "Economic Judgments in Congressional Voting," p. 499.
21. Kernell, "Negative Voting," p. 61.
22. Bruce E. Keith, David B. Magleby, Candice J. Nelson, Elizabeth Orr, Mark Westlye, and Raymond E. Wolfinger, "The Myth of the Independent Voter." (Paper delivered during the 1977 Annual Meeting of the American Political Science Association, Washington, D.C.).
23. Richard Brody, "Stability and Change in Party Identification: Presidential to Off-Years," (Paper delivered during the 1977 Annual Meeting of the American Political Science Association, Washington, D.C.).
24. Gerald H. Kramer, "Aggregate-Data Versus Survey-Research Findings on the Effects of Economic Conditions on Voting Behavior: Which Ones Would We Believe? Or, Is There Really Any Discrepancy?" (paper, California Institute of Technology, Pasadena, 1980).
25. Fiorina, "Short and Long-term Effects."
26. Brody, "Stability and Change."
27. Important contributions to this literature include Robert S. Erikson, "Malapportionment, Gerrymandering, and Party Fortunes in Congressional Elections," *American Political Science Review* 66 (1972): 1234–45; David R. Mayhew, "Congressional Eletions: The Case of the Vanishing Marginals," *Polity* 6 (1974): 295–317; John A. Ferejohn, "On the Decline of Competition in Congressional Elections," *American Political Science Review* 71 (1977): 166–76; Albert D. Cover and David R. Mayhew, "Congressional Dynamics and the Decline of Competitive Congressional Elections," in *Congress Reconsidered,* ed. Lawrence C. Dodd and Bruce I. Oppenheimer (New York: Praeger, 1977); and Albert D. Cover, "One Good Term Deserves Another: The Advantage of Incumbency in Congressional Elections," *American Journal of Political Science* 21 (1977): 523–42.
28. Walter Dean Burnham, "American Politics in the 1970's: Beyond Party?" in *The American Party Systems: Stages of Political Development,* ed. William Nisbet Chambers and Walter Dean Burnham, 2d ed. (New York: Oxford University Press, 1975) and "Insulation and Responsiveness in Congressional Elections," *Political Science Quarterly* 90 (1975): 411–35.
29. Donald E. Stokes and Warren E. Miller, "Party Government and the Saliency of Congress," *Public Opinion Quarterly* 26 (1962): 531–46.
30. Arseneau and Wolfinger, "Congressional Elections."
31. Gary C. Jacobson, *Money in Congressional Elections* (New Haven: Yale University Press, 1980), p. 12.
32. Ferejohn, "Competition in Congressional Elections," p. 171.
33. Alan I. Abramowitz, "Name Familiarity, Reputation, and the Incumbency Effect in a Congressional Election," *Western Political Quarterly* 28 (1975): 673–83.
34. Jacobson, *Money in Congressional Elections,* p. 16.
35. Thomas E. Mann, *Unsafe At Any Margin: Interpreting Congressional Elections* (Washington, D.C.: American Enterprise Institute for Public Policy Research, 1978), pp. 30–34 and 55–75.

36. See Thomas E. Mann and Raymond E. Wolfinger, "Candidates and Parties in Congressional Elections," (Paper delivered during the Annual Meeting of the American Political Science Association, Washington, D.C., August 31–September 3, 1979); Barbara Hinckley, "House Reelections and Senate Defeats: The Role of the Challenger," *British Journal of Political Science* (in press, 1980); Alan I. Abramowitz, "Electoral Accountability in 1978: A Comparison of Voting for U.S. Senator and Representative," (Paper delivered during the Annual Meeting of the American Political Science Association, Washington, D.C., August 31–September 3, 1979); Glenn R. Parker, "Incumbent Popularity and Congressional Elections," (Paper delivered during the Annual Meeting of the American Political Science Association, Washington, D.C., August 31–September 3, 1979); Gary C. Jacobson, "Congressional Elections, 1978: The Case of the Vanishing Challengers," (Paper delivered during the Conference on Congressional Elections, Rice University and the University of Houston, Houston, Tex. January 10–12, 1980).

37. The variables in table 2.1 are constructed as follows:

Respondent's vote	1 if Democrat; 0 if Republican
Party Identification	1 if strong, weak, or independent Democrat, 0 if independent independent, − 1 if strong, weak, or independent Republican
Democrat is incumbent	1 if Democrat is incumbent; 0 otherwise
Republican is incumbent	1 if Republican is incumbent; 0 otherwise
Familiarity with Democrat	2 if respondent recalls candidate's name;
Familiarity with Republican	1 if name is recognized but not recalled; 0 if name is not recognized or recalled
Likes something about Democrat	For each variable, 1 if respondent mentions anything liked (or disliked) about the candidate; 0 otherwise
Dislikes something about Democrat	
Likes something about Republican	
Dislikes something about Republican	

38. Note that the effect of incumbency per se is greatly diminished in the second equation. The regression coefficients for the incumbency variables are reduced by more than half, and they no longer differ significantly from zero. The impact of familiarity with the candidates is also substantially smaller. It is also worth noting that voters evaluate candidates primarily in terms of personal characteristics, job performance, and competence, with relatively few references to general policy positions and even fewer to specific policy stands; see Parker, "Incumbent Popularity and Congressional Elections."

39. Jacobson, "Congressional Elections, 1978," p. 14.

40. Hinckley, "House Reelections and Senate Defeats"; Abramowitz, "Electoral Accountability in 1978"; Mann and Wolfinger, "Candidates and Parties in Congressional Elections"; Jacobson, "Congressional Elections, 1978."

41. Some caution is advisable in using the 1978 NES/CPS Survey; the respondents seem inordinately fond of incumbents; for example, they overreport

voting for the incumbent by more than 10 percent. See Jacobson, "Congressional Elections, 1978," pp. 16–18.
42. Kramer, "U.S. Voting Behavior," p. 135.
43. Arcelus and Meltzer, "Congressional Elections," pp. 1235–36.
44. Bloom and Price, "Voter Response to Short-Run Economic Conditions," p. 1243.

CHAPTER 3

1. V. O. Key, Jr. (with the assistance of Milton Cummings), *The Responsible Electorate* (Cambridge: Harvard University Press, 1966), p. 7.
2. For a discussion of the evolution of the modern opportunity structure during the nineteenth century see Samuel Kernell, "Toward Understanding 19th Century Congressional Careers: Ambition, Competition, and Rotation," *American Journal of Political Science* 21 (1977):669–93 and "Congressional Careerism and the Emergence of a Political Career Structure" (Paper delivered during the meeting of the Social Science History Association, Cambridge, Mass. 1979).
3. Joseph A. Schlesinger, *Ambition and Politics: Political Careers in the United States* (Chicago: Rand McNally, 1966), chap. 6.
4. Thomas Kazee arrives at a similar conclusion in a study of decisions to run for Congress. See his "The Decision to Run for the U.S. Congress; Challenger Attitudes in the 1970's," *Legislative Studies Quarterly* 5 (1980): 79–100.
5. Gordon Black, "A Theory of Political Ambition: Career Choices and the Role of Structural Incentives," *American Political Science Review* 66 (1972): 144–59.
6. We argue in chapter 5 that the probability of attaining the collective goal of minimizing the loss of congressional seats affects the value some politicians place on the office and hence their strategic decision about running.
7. Kernell, "19th Century Congressional Careers"; William J. Keefe, *Parties, Politics, and Public Policy in America*, 2d ed. (Hinsdale, Ill.: Dryden Press, 1976), p. 39.
8. "Who Advised Truman?" *New York Times*, 6 January 1946, pt. 4, p. 7.
9. Cabell Phillips, "Republican's Outlook Called Best in 13 Years," *New York Times*, 24 February 1946, pt. 1, p. 31.
10. John H. Crider, "Brownell Favors New Stassen Plan," *New York Times*, 31 March 1946, pt. 1, p. 31.
11. Arthur Krock, "Confident Democrats Canvass 1960 Outlook," *New York Times*, 22 February 1958, pt. 4, p. 3.
12. "The Big Issue," *Newsweek*, 3 February 1958, p. 18.
13. Russell Baker, "G.O.P. Faces Hard Task," *New York Times*, 11 February 1962, pt. 4, p. 5.
14. Tom Wicker, "Both Sides Wary on House Races," *New York Times*, 28 April 1962, pt. 1, p. 69.
15. R. W. Apple, Jr., "Election Problems of the G.O.P. Assayed," *New York Times*, 10 February 1974, pt. 4, p. 3.

16. See, for example, "Republicans: Running Hard in Watergate's Shadow," *C.Q. Weekly Report* 32 (16 February 1974): 352–58.

17. George H. Gallup, *The Gallup Poll: Public Opinion 1935–1971* (New York: Random House, 1972), 2: 1161, 1210, 1221. The Gallup question was, "If elections for Congress were being held today, which party would you like to see win this state—the Republican Party or the Democratic Party?"

18. "Ike's Formula for '58 Elections: Help Business, Hold Peace Talks," *U.S. News and World Report*, 14 February 1958, p. 37. By May, 58 percent reported favoring the Democrats, prompting Gallup to observe that "not since 1936 had Democratic chances of taking overwhelming control of Congress seemed so good." See *Time*, 26 May 1958, p. 23.

19. Cabell Phillips, "G.O.P. Sure It Can Win in the House," *New York Times*, 16 June 1948, pt. 4, p. 7.

20. "Democratic Joy, Republican Gloom in Michigan's 5th," *C.Q. Weekly Report* 32 (23 February 1974): 493. Even a lost by-election may be taken as grounds for optimism. That of the Democrats in 1958 was "fortified by a hair-line Republican victory [in February, 1958] in a rural Minnesota congressional district that since 1893 has constantly elected Republicans by large margins" (Krock, "Confident Democrats," *New York Times*, 22 February 1958, pt. 4, p. 3).

21. "Running Hard in Watergate's Shadow," *C.Q. Weekly Report*, 32 (16 February 1974):353.

22. "Southern Republicans: Little Hope This Year," *C.Q. Weekly Report* 32 (October 26, 1974): 2959.

23. This effect was not confined to congressional candidates. A Republican official in Tennessee lamented that his party was only contesting 65 seats in the state legislature. "Good, attractive candidates just said this was not the year to run." Ibid., p. 2961.

24. Linda L. Fowler, "Candidate Perceptions of Electoral Coalitions: Limits and Possibilities" (Paper delivered during the Conference on Congressional Elections, Rice University and the University of Houston, Houston, Tex., January 10–12, 1980), p. 11.

25. Note that a difference remains when party is controlled, although it tends to be greater for Republicans than for Democrats.

26. State legislatures are the most frequent source of elective office experience for nonincumbent congressional candidates. National Republican leaders have recognized this explicitly and have contributed to state legislative campaigns with the acknowledged purpose of building up their pool of congressional talent.

27. Fowler, "Candidate Perceptions of Electoral Coalitions," p. 16.

CHAPTER 4

1. A more elaborate and thoroughly documented presentation of these ideas can be found in Gary C. Jacobson, *Money in Congressional Elections* (New Haven: Yale University Press, 1980), chap. 3.

2. See, for example, William P. Welch, "The Economics of Campaign Funds,"

Public Choice 25 (1976); James E. Zinser and Paul A. Dawson, "The Rationality of Indigenous Campaign Contributions" (Paper delivered during the 1977 Annual Meeting of the Public Choice Society, New Orleans, March 11–13, 1977).

3. See Jacobson, Money in Congressional Elections, pp. 113–23, for the full evidence.

4. W. P. Welch, "Patterns of Contributions: Economic Interest and Ideological Groups," in Political Finance, Sage Electoral Studies Yearbook, vol. 5, ed. Herbert E. Alexander, (Beverly Hills and London: Sage Publications, 1979), pp. 199–220.

5. "A Firm Organizes, Makes Political Voice Heard," Los Angeles Times, 12 May 1980.

6. The evidence is in Gary C. Jacobson, "The Pattern of Campaign Contributions to Candidates for the U.S. House of Representatives 1972–78," in An Analysis of the Impact of the Federal Election Campaign Act, 1972–1978, Report by the Campaign Finance Study Group to the Committee on House Administration of the U.S. House of Representatives (Cambridge, Mass.: Institute of Politics, John F. Kennedy School of Government, Harvard University, May, 1979), pp. 35–41.

7. David R. Mayhew, "Congressional Elections: The Case of the Vanishing Marginals," Polity 6 (1974): 298–301.

8. C.Q. Weekly Report 32 (16 February 1974): 352.

9. Ibid., p. 353.

10. Expenditures rather than contributions are listed because differences in regulations and methods of data collection among these elections make them more comparable figures. The pattern of expenditures depends heavily on the pattern of contributions in any case. If contributions are disaggregated by source, the same pattern appears in each.

11. The figures in table 4.1 also support, in summary fashion, several of the points made in the previous section. Incumbents obviously have an easier time raising money than do their challengers. And as we would expect, whether or not a nonincumbent candidate is facing an incumbent has an enormous effect on his ability to acquire campaign funds. Typically, the most expensive campaigns of all are for open seats.

12. See Jacobson, Money in Congressional Elections, pp. 84–85; 127–28.

13. Gary C. Jacobson, "The Effects of Campaign Spending in Congressional Elections," American Political Science Review 72 (1978): 470–78, and Money in Congressional Elections, chaps. 2, 5.

14. The challenger is estimated to gain approximatley 1 percentage point for each $10,000 (in 1972 dollars) spent on the campaign. Our discussion of contributor strategies raises the possibility that these estimates are subject to simultaneity bias; money not only generates votes, but the expectation of votes generates money. However, two-stage least-squares analysis of a simultaneous equation model of these relationships indicates that simultaneity bias is not a serious source of distortion. See Jacobson, Money in Congressional Elections, pp. 136–145.

15. David R. Mayhew, Congress: The Electoral Connection (New Haven: Yale University Press, 1974).

16. Direct evidence for this can be found in the connection between how much a candidate spends and how familiar he is to voters in the district. In all three elections for which requisite data are available (1972, 1974, and 1978), campaign spending by challengers and other nonincumbents is strongly related to how well they are known by voters. Only in 1974 is there any significant relationship between these two variables for incumbents, and even in that year nonincumbent spending had the greater effect. See Jacobson, *Money in Congressional Elections*, pp. 145–57 and "Congressional Elections 1978: The Case of the Vanishing Challengers," (Paper delivered during the Conference on Congressional Elections, Rice University and the University of Houston, Houston, Tex., January 10–12, 1980), pp. 8–9.

Campaign spending is important to both candidates in contests for open seats. It tends, however, to matter more to Republicans than to Democrats, which is not particularly surprising since fewer voters indentify themselves as Republicans. Expenditures are evidently more important to candidates who suffer from electoral handicaps of any kind.

17. The challenger's vote is measured as the percentage share of the two-party vote won by the challenger. The variables indicating whether or not the challenger is a Democrat or has held elective office are 1 if yes in either case, 0 if not. The strength of the challenger's party is measured as the percentage of the vote won by the challenger's party's candidate in the last election for this seat. Expenditures are measured in thousands of dollars. The sources for the data in these equations are given in Jacobson, *Money in Congressional Elections*, pp. 38–39 and 115.

18. One further observation is in order. Experience in the elective office is, on the evidence of equation 4.2, worth about 1.9 percent of the vote. But this measures only its direct effect. Much of its effect is in fact indirect; experienced candidates raise and spend substantially more money and this is where the advantage of experience is most apparent.

19. Gerald C. Wright, Jr., "Constituency Response to Congressional Behavior: The Impact of the House Judiciary Committee Impeachment Votes," *Western Political Quarterly* 30 (1977): 401–10.

20. David Johnston, "Leggett Likely to Win Despite Scandal," *Los Angeles Times*, 19 October 1976.

CHAPTER 5

1. Stephen Frantzich, "Opting Out: Retirement From the House of Representatives, 1966–1974," *American Politics Quarterly* 6 (1978): 251–73.

2. R. W. Apple, Jr., "Election Problems of G.O.P. Assayed," *New York Times*, 10 February 1974, pt. 4, p. 3.

3. That minority-party status may make the job less attractive can be found in the following twentieth-century retirement rates:

	Mean Percent Retiring	
	1896–1932	1934–1970
Democrats	11.9	3.5
Republicans	8.8	4.7

In both party systems the minority party congressmen retired at a marginally higher rate. Frantzich similarly reports that during the 1970s Republican congressmen were more likely to have "progressive" career ambitions while Democrats most evinced "static" ambitions ("Opting Out," pp. 112–14).

4. Nancy Skelton, "Wilson Will End Mystery Today on Congress Seat Held for 28 Years," *Los Angeles Times*, 18 January 1980.

5. More generally, as members near retirement the value of the office should be discounted with each election as the return on investment in the office becomes increasingly short-term.

6. The Democratic and Republican retirement series was compiled from the Inter-University Consortium for Political and Social Research's (ICPSR) "Biographical Characteristics of Members of the United States Congress, 1789–1977." The data was originally collected by Carroll R. McKibbin. Neither he nor the consortium bear any responsibility for the analyses or interpretations presented here. Unfortunately, these data do not identify the date and reason for a congressman's last departure from Congress. To compile overall partisan retirement rates for each Congress required that all congressmen who had interrupted careers or who subsequently served in the Senate had to be examined individually using the *Biographical Directory of the American Congress*, 5th ed.

7. Nelson Polsby, "The Institutionalization of the U.S. House of Representatives," *American Political Science Review* 68 (1969): 144–68 and Samuel Kernell, "Toward Understanding 19th Century Congressional Careers: Ambition, Competition, and Rotation," *American Journal of Political Science* 21 (1977): 669–93.

8. Kramer, "Short-Term Fluctuations in U.S. Voting Behavior"; Stigler, "General Economic Conditions and National Elections"; and Tufte, "Determinants of the Outcomes of Midterm Congressional Elections."

9. The exclusion of 1942 marginally improves most of the statistical relationships reported below.

10. The relationships are more impressive when one recognizes that the retirement rates exclude the South while the national vote totals include the South. To the degree that the congressional vote in that region was stable during the period, its inclusion in the vote totals serves to weaken the correlations but should not affect their direction.

11. Duff Spafford, "A Note on the 'Equilibrium' Division of the Vote," *American Political Science Review* 65 (1971): 180–83.

12. For example, the Democrats' hold on southern congressional seats has loosened much more slowly than might be expected from southern voting behavior in presidential elections or changes in party identification.

13. Following Tufte's and Converse's example the average or normal vote has been calculated by averaging the national congressional vote for the preceding eight elections. The difference in incumbency is the number of Republican incumbents seeking reelection minus the number of Democrats. See Phillip E. Converse, "The Concept of the Normal Vote," in Angus Campbell, Philip E. Converse, Warren Miller, and Donald Stokes, *Elections and the Political Order* (New York: Wiley, 1966): 9–39.

14. This finding matches the greater importance of candidate-related variables

over party identification in explaining the individual vote choice reported
in table 2.1.

CHAPTER 6

1. In analyzing variations in on- and off-year elections Kramer concludes,
   "that around one-third of the votes gained (or lost) because of the specific
   candidates and campaign tactics of the presidential race carry over to the
   congressional candidates of the same party" (p. 140).
2. James Bryce, *The American Commonwealth* (Norwood, Mass.: Macmillan
   and Co., 1913), p. 128 (emphasis added).
3. V. O. Key, Jr., *Politics, Parties and Pressure Groups* 5th ed., (New York:
   Thomas Y. Crowell, 1964), p. 567.
4. Tufte, "Determinants of the Outcomes of Midterm Congressional Elections,"
   pp. 817–18. Tufte omitted the 1942 midterm election because of distorting
   wartime economic controls.
5. See Tufte's caveat cited in chapter 2.
6. In testing our theory against Tufte's we are, of course, limited to elections
   for which presidential popularity ratings are available.
7. Unfortunately, the National Bureau of Economic Research's quarterly real
   income series begins in 1946 rather than 1945, the date needed to obtain
   change scores. This requires using the annual level for 1946 in both the
   spring and fall income series.
8. The revised estimates are also lower because adding 1974 and 1978 reduces
   the fit of the equation, even for Tufte's original specification of the real
   income variable. In both instances the equation overpredicts the degree of
   change in the vote attributable to short-run forces. Perhaps this is but one
   additional manifestation of the increased incumbency effect on congressional elections.
9. At least they think it does. An alternative explanation for these results is
   that congressional elites are convinced that economic conditions are important to voters but they are not nearly so certain about presidential popularity. Presidents' attempts to influence congressional elections directly
   have not been notably effective, regardless of their public standing. And the
   general effects of presidential popularity on election results have not always
   been obvious. A comment by a Republican politician interviewed in 1962
   is instructive: "The Democrats are whistling in the dark if they think Kennedy's popularity will affect Congressional races any more than Eisen-
   hower's did in 1958" ("Heating Up Mid-Term Campaigns," *Business Week*,
   26 May 1962, p. 467). It would be ironic if elites were influenced more
   strongly by their readings of economic conditions—which have little direct
   influence on voters—than by the president's popularity, which evidently
   does influence the voter.
10. Twenty percent by one estimate (Arseneau and Wolfinger, "Voting Behavior
    in Congressional Elections").
11. Samuel Kernell, "Explaining Presidential Popularity," *American Political
    Science Review* 72 (1978): 506–22; Samuel Kernell and Douglas A. Hibbs,

Jr., "A Critical Threshold Model of Presidential Popularity," and Douglas A. Hibbs, Jr. and Nicholas Vasilatos, "Macroeconomic Performance and Mass Political Support in the United States and Great Britain," in *Contemporary Political Economy*, ed. Douglas A. Hibbs, Jr. and Heino Fassbender (New York: North Holland, 1981), pp. 49–72 and 31–48, respectively.

12. There are two alternative interpretations available for equation 6.3 which are less generous to economic voting theory. The first argues that the fall estimates may also reflect structural features of the electoral setting. During the fall campaign, for example, a favorable political climate may make it easier for the candidate to sustain campaign contributions and volunteer participation. Local activists respond much as voters respond to their evaluations of the president's job performance in contributing to campaigns. The second alternative explanation is unabashedly ad hoc. (Normally, this would make it less attractive, but as our degrees of freedom approach that of a case study we should keep in mind the academic aphorism that anecdote is the singular form of data.) The main problem of the spring popularity term is the 1974 election with President Nixon's popularity hovering around 26 percent for most of the spring. With the economy also in poor shape Nixon's popularity grossly overpredicts the decline of the Republican vote that year. This extreme case also means that the spring popularity variable tends to underpredict the vote for the remaining eight elections. The problem, we suspect, is that elite responses are less elastic at extremes of short-term conditions. Deleting the 1974 election and rerunning equation 6.3 produces a much improved estimate for spring popularity generally, at the expense of the fall estimates.

CHAPTER 7

1. Christopher Buchanan, "Modest GOP Congressional Gains Expected," *C.Q. Weekly Report* 38 (1 November 1980): 3242.
2. Christopher Buchanan, "Senators Face Tough Re-election Odds," *C.Q. Weekly Report* 38 (5 April 1980): 905–09.
3. Gary Jacobson, *Money in Congressional Elections*, (New Haven: Yale University Press, 1980) p. 133.
4. See Mann and Wolfinger, "Candidates and Parties in Congressional Elections"; Hinckley, "House Reelections and Senate Defeats"; Abramowitz, "Electoral Accountability in 1978."
5. "The Outlook: Senate, House and Governors," *C.Q. Weekly Report* 38 (11 October 1980): 2986–3086.
6. Ibid.
7. See Mann, *Unsafe at Any Margin*, pp. 82–87. The election returns are from nearly complete, unofficial returns in *C.Q. Weekly Report* 38 (8 November 1980): 3338–45.
8. The $75,000 cutoff level is, of course, somewhat arbitrary; it could be raised or lowered substantially without affecting the point to be made.
9. The third winner in the lower right quadrant, Duncan Hunter, who upset veteran Democratic incumbent Lionel Van Deerlin, financed the early part

of his campaign by loaning it $114,000 of his own money. This does not appear in the preliminary FEC report, so he remains, for consistency's sake, in the "weak candidacy" category.

10. This reflects the successful Republican strategy, discussed below, of going after seats held by senior House Democrats.

11. *Gallup Opinion Index* 177 (April–May 1980):23.

12. Ibid., p. 35; *Gallup Opinion Index* 175 (February 1980):13.

13. The pool ratio figures for 1980 make the same point and, as usual, a much higher proportion of candidates for open seats have held elective office: 68 percent of the Democrats, 45 percent of the Republicans. Most Senate challengers of both parties were similarly experienced: 72 percent of the Democrats and 67 percent of the Republicans.

14. "Congressional Retirements Down from Previous Years, Expected to Increase in 1982," *C.Q. Weekly Report* 38 (2 August 1980): 2172.

15. Larry Light, "Democrats May Lose Edge in Contributions from PACs," *C.Q. Weekly Report* 38 (2 November 1980): 3409.

16. Ibid. Five other PACs listed in the *Weekly Report* distributed their money more evenly among Democrats and Republicans; not surprisingly, most of this money went to incumbents.

17. Christopher Buchanan, "Republicans Make Substantial House Gains," *C.Q. Weekly Report* 38 (8 November 1980): 3317.

18. The same idea has been expressed in informal, postelection discussions by Thomas Mann and David Mayhew.

CHAPTER 8

1. For an example of vacancy-based mobility, see Harrison White, *Chains of Opportunity* (Cambridge: Harvard University Press, 1970).

2. The 1980 election witnessed two such cases when a neo-Nazi and a Klansman won a Republican and Democratic congressional primary, respectively. In the latter, nationally more prominent case, Tom Metzger, the California state head of the Ku Klux Klan won his nomination (Calif., 43rd) against two faint-hearted rivals who together spent under $5000. Just their being on the ballot, however, was sufficient to so split the anti-Klan vote that Metzger won the primary with little more than one-third of the popular vote. In November he was soundly defeated, of course, by the incumbent Republican, Clare Burgener, but this did not detract from Metzger's resounding success in generating national publicity.

3. Whether or not elite strategies were as important in structuring the congressional vote in earlier decades as they are now is an intriguing question; we cannot answer it here, since our most comprehensive evidence is limited to the 1970s; one of us (Jacobson) is currently pursuing the question under National Science Foundation Grant No. SES 80-07557.

4. Morris P. Fiorina, "Economic Retrospective Voting in American National Elections: A Micro-Analysis," *American Journal of Political Science* 22 (1978):440.

5. "The 1974 Elections: Integrity is the Universal Subject," *C.Q. Weekly Report* 32 (23 February 1974): 391.
6. *C.Q. Weekly Report* 32 (2 March 1974): 544.
7. *C.Q. Weekly Report* 36 (25 March 1978): 754.
8. See Gary C. Jacobson, "Congressional Elections, 1978: The Case of the Vanishing Challengers," (Paper delivered during the Conference on Congressional Elections, Rice University and the University of Houston, Houston, Tex., January 10–12, 1980).

EPILOGUE

1. This equation is based on the data in Tufte, *Political Control of the Economy*, p. 111, with data for 1978 added; we use it rather than the modified version of the referendum equation we developed in chapter 6 because Tufte's original equation is widely recognized as standard in the literature.
2. An alternative seats/votes equation offered by Douglas Hibbs would convert this vote into a Republican loss of 65 seats. See his "President Reagan's Mandate from 1980 Elections: A Shift to the Right?" *American Politics Quarterly* 10 (October 1982):411.
3. "The 1982 National Vote," *C.Q. Weekly Report* 41 (19 February, 1983):387.
4. For details, see Gary C. Jacobson, "Congressional Campaign Finance and the Revival of the Republican Party," in Dennis Hale, ed., *The United States Congress: Proceedings of the Thomas P. O'Neill, Jr., Symposium* (Chestnut Hill, Mass.: Boston College, 1982), pp. 313–30.
5. "GOP Earmarks $63 Million for '82," *San Diego Union*, 17 January 1982, p. 18.
6. "More Voters to Back GOP Candidates, Survey Finds," *Los Angeles Times*, 24 May 1981, pt. 1, p. 11.
7. Adam Clymer, "GOP Worried about Impact of Job Figures," *New York Times*, 15 January 1982, p. 9.
8. Adam Clymer, "Those Who Recruit Candidates Say the Parties Are Running about Even," *New York Times*, 8 March 1982, p. 4.
9. Lynda Du Val, RNCC, telephone interview, 9 January 1982.
10. Clymer, "Parties Are Running about Even," p. 4.
11. Adam Clymer, "GOP Recruiting in Missouri for House Contests," *New York Times*, 13 February 1982, p. 8.
12. From information in "Special Report: The 1982 Election," supplement to *C.Q. Weekly Report* 40 (9 October 1982):2477–2612.
13. See Gary C. Jacobson, "Strategic Politicians and Congressional Elections, 1946–1978" (paper delivered during the Annual Meeting of the American Political Science Association, New York, 3–6 September 1981).
14. Richard E. Cohen, "Congress: Control at Stake," *National Journal*, 9 January 1982, p. 66.
15. Richard E. Cohen, "Giving till It Hurts: 1982 Campaign Prompts New Look at Financing Races," *National Journal*, 18 December 1982, p. 2145.
16. Steven V. Roberts, "G.O.P. Challengers Get Low Priority," *New York Times*, 16 September 1982, pt. 2, p. 10.
17. Dennis Farney, "Business PACs Decide to Go on the Defense," *Wall Street Journal*, 10 June 1982, p. 25.

18. Ibid., p. 43.
19. Albert R. Hunt, "An Inside Look at Politicians Hustling PACs," *Wall Street Journal*, 1 October 1982, p. 43.
20. Roberts, "G.O.P. Challengers," p. 10.
21. Cohen, "Congress," p. 66.
22. Clymer, "GOP Recruiting," p. 8.
23. Clymer, "Parties Are Running about Even," p. 4.
24. Adam Clymer, "Light Wallets Weigh Heavily on Democrats," *New York Times*, 17 October 1982, p. E4.
25. Roberts, "Congress," p. 66.
26. A formally identical clash of interests also limits the ability of parties to maximize their gains through a partisan gerrymander; see Bruce Cain, *The Reapportionment Puzzle* (Berkeley: University of California Press, forthcoming).
27. See Gary C. Jacobson, "Money in the 1980 Congressional Elections" (paper delivered at the Annual Meeting of the Midwest Political Science Association, Milwaukee, 28 April–1 May, 1982).
28. Cohen, "Giving till It Hurts," p. 2145.
29. Includes only data reported through 13 October 1982. See "1982 Congressional Races Set Record Spending," Federal Election Commission news release, 7 January 1983.
30. Dennis Farney and Brooks Jackson, "GOP Channels Money into Those Campaigns That Need It Most," *Wall Street Journal*, 19 October 1982, p. 1.
31. Adam Clymer, "Campaign Funds Called a Key to Outcome of House Races," *New York Times*, 5 November 1982, p. B10; Cohen, "Giving till It Hurts," p. 2146.
32. Jacobson, *Money in Congressional Elections*, p. 46.
33. Thomas E. Mann and Norman J. Ornstein, "Election '82: The Voters Send a Message," *Public Opinion* 5 (December/January 1983), p. 7.
34. Rob Gurwitt and Tom Watson, "Democrats Recoup State Legislative Losses," *C.Q. Weekly Report* 40 (13 November 1982), p. 2849.

Index